REBELLION vs. OBEDIENCE

It's Your Choice

By: Diane Bernardin

RESOURCES

ALL SCRIPTURES TAKEN FROM THE NKJV
Thomas Nelson Publisher

Library of Congress
1-7665805151
ISBN# 978-0-9889500-8-5
Printed in the United States of America
Published through CrossSounds Ministries Media
Contact: Dianeb22000@gmail.com

TABLE OF CONTENTS

FOREWARD

From the very beginning of the creation of man, God desired to have fellowship with created beings. He contains the power to create us in any fashion He desired. He could easily have made us programmed to worship and adore Him like the robots that the artificial intelligence scientists have designed and created today. He is God.

So why would He create a species called human beings, forming them from the dirt in the ground, along with water; breathe His own breath into their lungs and allow them the ability to live? Why would He give them an incredible gift of a beautiful planet that they could safely live on, give them all the plants and food they would need, and gift them with creative capacity to form new inventions over time that would make sensational changes to their world?

Furthermore, why would this creator desire to have fellowship with His creation? He gave them the most incredible gift He could give and intended for them to use it wisely. That gift is something called a choice. Why? Because He wants man to desire to find Him, desire to know Him and choose seek Him first in this life, to know His will and desire for them to serve Him as the one true God who created them because He loves them. Love demands a choice. Love is the greatest description of who He is and He states that We were created in His image, His likeness and we were given a mind to think and make choices that He desires for us or we desire, but as you read the scriptures, you will see the results that came for the right and wrong choices.

I want to find many of them, so you can read the word yourself and make some very important choices regarding your life. We all make our own choices and His desire for us is His will; His will was written in the bible. It is a manual to guide every one of our lives. He covers the most important areas of our lives throughout the book and contains the most incredible discovery of who He is,

what He desires, how He feels (yes, He has emotions), instructions of life while here on this earth and our eternal future together with Him. He also shares the alternative consequences that are available to those who choose something else. The choice is definitely yours and He respects that. My prayer for you as you are reading this book, is that you will make the choice that He desires for you. It was written for you. There is a battle that arose to hinder our choices. It will clearly be seen from Genesis to Revelation. It is called rebellion and disobedience. It will try to influence you all your life. After many years where rebellion and disobedience ruled my life, I have made my choice to live for Him and obey His word here and to forever live with Him in eternity. His greatest desire is that you choose life!

"I call heaven and earth as witnesses today against you, *that* I have set before you **life** and death, blessing and cursing; therefore **choose life**, that both you and your descendants may live;" **Deut. 30:19**

"And if it seems evil to you to serve the **Lord**, **choose** for yourselves this day whom you will serve, whether the gods which your fathers served that *were* on the other side of the River, or the gods of the Amorites, in whose land you dwell. But as for me and my house, we will serve the **Lord**." **Jos. 24:15**

A WORD OF THANKS

Special thanks to my patient husband, Michel Bernardin for his love, encouragement and prayer support in the writing of this book.

Special thanks to my dear sister Sharon, who has been my prayer partner for decades and has faithfully prayed for my completion of this book.

Special thanks to my dear friends who prayed for me in the writing of this book: Lillian Garrett, Millie Smith. Bishop Chris Johnson, Pastor Connie Ingram and Joyce McGuire. I am so grateful for each one of you and pray the Lord's blessings are abundantly poured out to you all!

INTRODUCTION

MEET THE THIEF

You can feel it rising up on the inside of you. This sometimes silent, but incredible inner war is going on. You want to scream at someone who is telling you to do something another way than you planned. You made all your plans, you had every detail settled in your mind of how you were going to do it. You were so excited about starting it and set aside everything else to give this top priority. Then the time arrives to share your plan, your vision and dream with someone you sincerely trust and you can't wait for their response. You are so convinced they will see what you see and stand behind you with encouragement and applause, with the same great anticipation that you carry. Then it happens. They start to give reasons why this will not work and start to impart the way they would do it. Before the conversation ends, they have torn your vision down to nothing but an idea that you conjured up in your head that has no worth or possibility. The dream fades, and you walk away empty. You want to say, "You do not understand how long I worked on this dream, how can you respond in such a negative way?"

All at once, an inner thought arises. Then this secret counsel comes to you: "They are just negative. Don't listen to them. They don't know what they're talking about. You don't have to listen to them. Just do it and they'll see and you'll prove to them that you had a great idea. Who do they think they are telling you the way you should do it? Why did you ever share it with them? What a waste of time. Just do it yourself. You can't trust them or anyone!"

So the **dream stealer, the thief** comes to oppose all your plans and now his friends: fear, doubt, anger and confusion start to appear on the scene. Why? The thief has been ordered a strategic assignment against your life. You must make a choice that will determine the outcome of your life and stop him. The choice is yours.

It all started in the garden. Please read on.

*"The thief does not come except to **steal**, and to **kill**, and to **destroy**. I have come that they may have life, and that they may have it more abundantly."* **Jn. 10:10**

*"Be sober, be vigilant; because your adversary the devil walks about **like a roaring lion**, seeking whom he may devour."* **1 Pet. 5:8**

WE HAVE AN INTERCESSOR

And the Lord said, "Simon, Simon! Indeed, Satan has asked for you, that he may sift you as wheat. But I have prayed for you, that your faith should not fail; and when you have returned to Me, strengthen your brethren." **Luke 22:31-32**

THE LORD HAS GREAT PLANS FOR YOUR LIFE:

"For I know the thoughts that I think toward you, says the Lord, thoughts of peace and not of evil, to give you a future and a hope." **Jer. 29:11**

There is a common thread that is found in the word of God. These truths that you are about to read are astounding. They have been washed away and disregarded by some in the body of Christ. You said in Your word that heaven and earth would pass away, but Your word will NEVER pass away. Lord, allow Your people to see Your heart as I have. May we be forever impacted and become willing and surrendered vessels who humble themselves before a Mighty and Glorious God who reigns forever in Jesus' name I pray, amen.

"My people are destroyed for lack of knowledge. Because you have forgotten the law of Your God, I also will forget your children." **Hos. 4:6**

CHAPTER 1

WHO IS LUCIFER?

Lucifer was a created angel named "day star" or "son of the morning" who was beautiful, was full of wisdom and was given the highest rank as a worship leader in Heaven. He was cast out of the mountain of God when iniquity was found in him. (Rebellion and Disobedience)

The **Mountain of God (Mt. Horeb or Mt. Sinai)** is talked about in **Exodus 3**. It's the place where the Lord drew Moses to Himself and appeared to him. The place where He wrote His Commandments for His people, with His own finger. The place of His dwelling that a cloud covered. It was the place of His inheritance to those who served Him. It was the place of instruction. It was located in the wilderness of Sanai, it is believed. The sanctuary which the Lord's hands had established. It was a mountain of holiness and anyone touching it would die. They witnessed thunderings, lightning flashes, the sound of the trumpet and the mountain smoking. It caused great fear in the people which kept them from going near it. In **Rev. 21:10** the Lord reveals to John the great city of the New Jerusalem from a high mountain, which he is carried away to in the Spirit.

Ezek 28:11-19 "Moreover the word of the Lord came to me, saying, "Son of man, take up a lamentation for the king of Tyre, and say to him, 'Thus says the Lord God:

"You *were* the seal of perfection, Full of wisdom and perfect in beauty. You were in Eden, the garden of God; Every precious stone *was* your covering: The sardius, topaz, and diamond, beryl, onyx, and jasper, sapphire, turquoise, and emerald with gold. The workmanship of your timbrels and pipes was prepared for you on the day you were created.

"You *were* the anointed cherub who covers; I established you; **You were on the holy mountain of God;** You walked back and forth in the midst of fiery stones. You *were* perfect in your ways from the day you were created, till iniquity was found in you. "By the abundance of your trading you became filled with violence **within**, and you sinned; Therefore I cast you as a profane thing **out of the mountain of God**; and I destroyed you, O covering cherub, from the midst of the fiery stones.
"Your heart was lifted up **because of your beauty**; You corrupted your wisdom for the sake of your splendor; I cast you to the ground, I laid you before kings, That they might gaze at you.
"You defiled your sanctuaries by the multitude of your iniquities, By the iniquity of your trading; Therefore I brought fire from your midst; It devoured you, And I turned you to ashes upon the earth; In the sight of all who saw you. All who knew you among the peoples are astonished at you; You have become a horror, and *shall be* no more forever."

"Your pomp is brought down to Sheol, and the sound of your stringed instruments; The maggot is spread under you, and worms cover you.' "How you are fallen from heaven, O Lucifer, son of the morning! How you are cut down to the ground, you who weakened the nations! For you have said in your heart: **'I will ascend into heaven, I will exalt my throne above the stars of God; I will also sit on the mount of the congregation On the farthest sides of the north; I will ascend above the heights of the clouds, I will be like the Most High.'**

Yet you shall be brought down to Sheol, to the lowest depths of the Pit." Those who see you will gaze at you, and consider you, saying: '**Is this the man who made the earth tremble, who shook kingdoms, who made the world as a wilderness and destroyed its cities, who did not open the house of his prisoners?**' Who made the world as a wilderness and destroyed its cities, who did not open the house of his prisoners?' "All the kings of the nations, all of them, sleep in glory, everyone in his own house; but you are cast out of your grave like an abominable branch, like the garment of those who are slain, thrust through with a sword, who go down to the stones of the pit, like a corpse trodden underfoot." **Isaiah 14:11-19**

He has been given several names in scripture: Lucifer, (**Isa. 14:11**) Beelzebub, (**Mat. 12:24**) The King of Tyre, (**Ezek. 28**) Satan,(**Job 1:6**) the Serpent, (**Gen. 3:1**) Leviathan (**Isa. 27:1**) the devil (**Mat. 13:39**) and the great dragon (**Rev. 12:17**).

He tempted Jesus in the desert and promised him all the kingdoms of the world if He would just bow down and worship him. **Luk. 4:5**
He entered and inhabited the heart of Judas to betray Jesus. **Luk. 22:3**
He violently empowers the soldiers to mock and beat Jesus, then to crucify Him on the cross. **Jn.19:16**
He empowers the Antichrist, the Beast and the False Prophet in the book of Revelation. **Rev. 12:7-9**

<u>The greatest news of all</u>: One day he will be totally defeated and thrown into the Lake of Fire, where he is tormented forever along with all who serve him and have received his mark. **Rev. 20:10**

CHAPTER 2
WHAT IS REBELLION?

Webster's definition of the word rebellion is: opposition to one in authority or dominance. Open, armed and usually unsuccessful defiance of or resistance to an established government.
It is a person who refuses allegiance to, resists or rises in arms against the government or ruler of his or her country. We see this sin in operation every day in our world today.
It is **disobedience** against those placed in authority over us and it is sin. It is lawlessness as we become our own rulers and do things only **our way**. We do not like anyone telling us what to do. We are encouraged to pray for our governmental leaders every day.
"Let every soul be subject to the governing authorities. **For there is no authority except from God, and the authorities that exist are appointed by God. Therefore whoever resists the authority resists the ordinance of God, and those who resist will bring judgment on themselves**. For rulers are not a terror to good works, but to evil. Do you want to be unafraid of the authority? Do what is good, and you will have praise from the same. For he is God's minister to you for good. But if you do evil, be afraid; for he does not bear the sword in vain; for he is God's minister, an avenger to *execute* wrath on him who practices evil. Therefore *you* must be subject, not only because of wrath but also for conscience' sake. For because of this you also pay taxes, for they are God's ministers attending continually to this very thing; therefore to all their due: taxes to whom taxes *are due,* customs to whom customs, fear to whom fear, honor to whom honor." **Rom. 13:1-7**

The rule of the Kingdom of Heaven should be the most important governmental rule of our lives. We serve and honor the King of Kings and Lord of Lords, Jesus Christ ruler of Heaven and Earth.

He desires our **obedience** more than any sacrifice we think we can offer to him.
"Let God arise, Let His enemies be scattered; Let those also who hate Him flee before Him. As smoke is driven away, So drive *them* away; As wax melts before the fire, *So* let the wicked perish at the presence of God. But let the righteous be glad; Let them rejoice before God; Yes, let them rejoice exceedingly.

Sing to God, sing praises to His name; Extol Him who rides on the clouds, By His name Yah, and rejoice before Him. A father of the fatherless, a defender of widows, *is* God in His holy habitation. God sets the solitary in families; He brings out those who are bound into prosperity; **But the rebellious dwell in a dry land**." **Ps. 68:1-6**

REBELLION BEGAN IN THE GARDEN

"Now the serpent was more cunning than any beast of the field which the Lord God had made. And he said to the woman, "**Has God indeed said**, 'You shall not eat of every tree of the garden'?" And the woman said to the serpent, "We may eat the fruit of the trees of the garden; but of the fruit of the tree which *is* in the midst of the garden, **God has said, 'You shall not eat it, nor shall you touch it, lest you die.' "** Then the serpent said to the woman, "You will not surely die. For God knows that in the day you eat of it your eyes will be opened, and **you will be like God, knowing good and evil**."

So when the woman saw that the tree *was* good for food, that it *was* pleasant to the eyes, and a tree desirable to make *one* wise, she took of its fruit and ate. She also gave to her husband with her, and he ate. Then the eyes of both of them were opened, and they knew that they *were* naked; and they sewed fig leaves together and made themselves coverings. And they **heard the sound of the Lord God** walking in the garden in the cool of the day, and Adam and his wife hid themselves from the presence of the Lord God among the trees of the garden.

Then the Lord God called to Adam and said to him, "Where *are* you?" So he said, "I heard Your voice in the garden, and I was afraid because I was naked; and I hid myself." And He said, "Who told you that you *were* naked? Have you eaten from the tree of which I commanded you that you should not eat?"

Then the man said, "**The woman whom You gave *to be* with me, she gave me of the tree, and I ate.**" And the Lord God said to the woman, "What *is* this you have done?" The woman said, "**The serpent <u>deceived</u> me, and I ate**." So the **Lord God said to the serpent**:

"Because you have done this, **You *are* cursed** more than all cattle, And more than every beast of the field; **<u>On your belly you shall go</u>**, and you shall eat dust all the days of your life. and I will put enmity between you and the woman, and between your seed and her Seed; He shall bruise your head, and you shall bruise His heel."

To the **woman** He said: "**I will greatly multiply your sorrow and your conception; In pain you shall bring forth children; Your desire *shall be* for your husband, And he shall rule over you.**"

Then to **Adam** He said, "Because **you have heeded the voice of your wife**, and have eaten from the tree of which I **commanded**

you, saying, 'You shall not eat of it':

"Cursed *is* the ground for your sake; In toil you shall eat of it All the days of your life. Both thorns and thistles it shall bring forth for you,
And you shall eat the herb of the field. In the sweat of your face you shall eat bread
Till you return to the ground, For out of it you were taken; For dust you are,
And to dust you shall return."
And Adam called his wife's name Eve, because she was the mother of all living. Also for Adam and his wife the Lord God made tunics of skin, and **clothed them**. Then the Lord God said, **"Behold, the man has become like one of Us, to know good and evil. And now, lest he put out his hand and take also of the tree of life, and eat, and live forever"— therefore the Lord God sent him out of the garden of Eden to till the ground from which he was taken. So He drove out the man; and He placed cherubim at the east of the garden of Eden, and a flaming sword which turned every way, to guard the way to the tree of life." Gen. 3:1-24**

This sin of rebellion and disobedience cost Adam and Eve a great price: the provision of God, the protection of God and a spiritual doorway that was opened and the law of sin and death began to rule in their generational lineage. The choice was made, and we can see the results: Sin separating us from a holy God.

CHAPTER 3

GENERATIONAL REBELLION AND DISOBEDIENCE

CAIN

Now Adam knew Eve his wife, and she conceived and bore Cain, and said, "I have acquired a man from the Lord." Then she bore again, this time his brother Abel. Now Abel was a **keeper of sheep**, but Cain was a tiller of the ground. And in the process of time it came to pass that Cain brought an offering of the fruit of the ground to the Lord. Abel also brought of the **firstborn of his flock and of their fat. And the Lord respected Abel and his offering**, but He did not respect Cain and his offering. And Cain was **very angry, and his countenance fell**. So the Lord said to Cain, **"Why are you angry? And why has your countenance fallen? <u>If you do well</u>**, will you not be accepted? And **<u>if you do not do well</u>, sin lies at the door. And its desire *is* for you, but <u>you should rule over it."</u>**

Now Cain talked with Abel his brother; and it came to pass, when they were in the field, that Cain rose up against Abel his brother and killed him. Then the Lord said to Cain, "Where *is* Abel your brother?" He said, "I do not know. *Am* I my brother's keeper?" And He said, **"What have you done? The voice of your brother's blood cries out to Me from the ground. So now you *are* cursed from the earth, which has opened its mouth to receive your brother's blood from your hand. When you till the ground, it shall no longer yield its strength to you. A fugitive and a vagabond you shall be on the earth."**

And Cain said to the Lord, "My punishment *is* greater than I can bear! Surely You have driven me out this day from the face of the ground; **I shall be hidden from Your face**; I shall be a fugitive and a vagabond on the earth, and it will happen *that* anyone who finds me will kill me."

And the Lord said to him, "Therefore, whoever kills Cain, vengeance shall be taken on him sevenfold." And the Lord **set a mark** on Cain, lest anyone finding him should kill him." **Gen. 4:15**

What is so amazing to me in this passage, is even though Cain fails his test of obedience, when he cries to the Lord for mercy, the Lord sets His mark upon him with an a vengeance of sevenfold. What mercy was granted him from the Lord. The Lord released His wisdom and truth: sin lies at the door, its desire is for you, you should rule over it. A way of escape was provided.

HAM (SON OF NOAH)

Now the sons of Noah who went out of the ark were Shem, Ham, and Japheth. And Ham *was* the father of Canaan. These three *were* the sons of Noah, and from these the whole earth was populated. And Noah began *to be* a farmer, and he planted a vineyard. Then he drank of the wine and was drunk, and became uncovered in his tent. And Ham, the father of Canaan, **saw the nakedness of his father, and told his two brothers outside**. But Shem and Japheth took a garment, laid *it* on both their shoulders, and **went backward and covered the nakedness of their father. Their faces *were* turned away, and they did not**

<u>see their father's nakedness</u>. So Noah awoke from his wine, and <u>knew what his younger son had done to him</u>. Then he said: "**Cursed *be* Canaan; A servant of servants he shall be to his brethren**." And he said: "Blessed *be* the Lord, the God of Shem, and may Canaan be his servant. May God enlarge Japheth, and may he dwell in the tents of Shem; and may Canaan be his servant." **Gen 9:25**

It is very clear in this passage that the blessings of God went to the obedient generation and rebellion and disobedience caused Ham's generation to be cursed. This generational sin has continued to be passed on today.

<u>NIMROD</u>

Cush begot Nimrod; he began to be a mighty one on the earth. He was a mighty hunter before the Lord; therefore it is said, "Like Nimrod the mighty hunter before the Lord." **Gen. 10:8-9**

"Now the whole earth had one language and one speech. And it came to pass, as they journeyed from the east, that they found a plain in the land of Shinar, and they dwelt there. Then they said to one another, "Come, let us make bricks and bake *them* thoroughly." They had brick for stone, and they had asphalt for mortar. And they said, "Come, let us <u>build ourselves a city, and a tower whose top *is* in the heavens; let us make a name for ourselves, lest we be scattered abroad over the face of the whole earth."</u>

But the Lord came down to see the city and the tower which the sons of men had built. And the Lord said, "**Indeed the people *<u>are</u>***

one and they all have one language, and this is what they begin to do; now nothing that they propose to do will be withheld from them. Come, let Us go down and there confuse their language, that they may not understand one another's speech." So the Lord scattered them abroad from there over the face of all the earth, and they ceased building the city. Therefore its name is called Babel, because there the Lord confused the language of all the earth; and from there the Lord scattered them abroad over the face of all the earth." **Gen. 11:1-9**

Here we see Nimrod, the descendant of Ham, Noah's son, **repeating the same sin of rebellion and disobedience**. He **decides** to gather everyone together in unity, to build a tower of self-rule, with hearts of self exaltation and pride, where they were in charge of everything, as if to challenge God. They had agreement for an evil purpose and the Lord saw it and confused their language to scatter them. The sins of the father visit the generations following **unless** someone stands in the gap and repents.

MIRIAM AND AARON

"Then Miriam and Aaron spoke against Moses because of the Ethiopian woman whom he had married; for he had married an Ethiopian woman. So they said, "Has the Lord indeed spoken only through Moses? Has He not spoken through us also?" And the Lord heard *it.* (Now the man Moses *was* **very humble, more than all men who *were* on the face of the earth.**)

Suddenly the Lord said to Moses, Aaron, and Miriam, "Come out, you three, to the tabernacle of meeting!" So the three came out.

Then the Lord came down in the pillar of cloud and stood *in* the door of the tabernacle, and called Aaron and Miriam. And they both went forward. Then He said,

"Hear now My words: If there is a prophet among you, *I*, the Lord, make Myself known to him in a vision; I speak to him in a dream. Not so with My servant Moses; He *is* faithful in all My house. I speak with him face to face, Even plainly, and not in dark sayings; And he sees the form of the Lord. Why then were you not afraid to speak against My servant Moses?" So the anger of the Lord was aroused against them, and He departed. And when the cloud departed from above the tabernacle, suddenly Miriam *became* leprous, as *white as* snow. Then Aaron turned toward Miriam, and there she was, a leper. So Aaron said to Moses, "Oh, my lord! Please do not lay *this* sin on us, in which we have done foolishly and in which we have sinned. Please do not let her be as one dead, whose flesh is half consumed when he comes out of his mother's womb!"

So Moses cried out to the Lord, saying, "Please heal her, O God, I pray!"

Then the Lord said to Moses, "If her father had but spit in her face, would she not be shamed seven days? Let her be shut out of the camp seven days, and afterward she may be received *again*." So Miriam was shut out of the camp seven days, and the people did not journey till Miriam was brought in *again*. And afterward the people moved from Hazeroth and camped in the Wilderness of Paran." **Num. 12:1-15**

The rebellion of Miriam and Aaron coming against the anointed man of God Moses produced a disease upon Miriam called **leprosy** (the curse of sickness was released for rebellion). Aaron repented in fear and **Moses cried out for mercy on behalf of both of them**. What a heart of humility and forgiveness Moses had. When God has His hand upon a minister and positions them in ministry, we must never challenge them, as that action will result in an open door for disease to come.

KORAH, DATHAN AND ABIRAM

"Now Korah the son of Izhar, the son of Kohath, the son of Levi, with Dathan and Abiram the sons of Eliab, and On the son of Peleth, sons of Reuben, took *men;* and they rose up before Moses with some of the children of Israel, two hundred and fifty leaders of the congregation, representatives of the congregation, men of renown. **They gathered together against Moses and Aaron, and said to them, "*You take* too much upon yourselves, for all the congregation *is* holy, every one of them, and the Lord *is* among them. Why then do you exalt yourselves above the assembly of the Lord?"**

So when Moses heard *it,* **he fell on his face**; and he spoke to Korah and all his company, saying, "Tomorrow morning **the Lord will show who *is* His and *who is* holy, and will cause *him* to come near to Him. That one whom He chooses He will cause to come near to Him**. Do this: Take censers, Korah and all your company; put fire in them and put incense in them before the Lord tomorrow, and it shall be *that* the man whom the Lord chooses *is* the holy one. *You take* too much upon yourselves, you sons of Levi!"

Then Moses said to Korah, "Hear now, you sons of Levi: *Is it* a small thing to you that the God of Israel has separated you from the congregation of Israel, to bring you near to Himself, to do the work of the tabernacle of the Lord, and to stand before the congregation to serve them; and that He has brought you near *to Himself,* you and all your brethren, the sons of Levi, with you? And are you seeking the priesthood also? Therefore you and all your company *are* gathered together **against the Lord**. And what *is* Aaron that you complain against him?"

And Moses sent to call Dathan and Abiram the sons of Eliab, but they said, "We will not come up! *Is it* a small thing that you have brought us up out of a land flowing with milk and honey, to kill us in the wilderness, that you should keep acting like a prince over us? Moreover you have not brought us into a land flowing with milk and honey, nor given us inheritance of fields and vineyards. Will you put out the eyes of these men? We will not come up!"

Then Moses was very angry, and said to the Lord, "Do not respect their offering. I have not taken one donkey from them, nor have I hurt one of them."

And Moses said to Korah, "Tomorrow, you and all your company be present before the Lord—you and they, as well as Aaron. Let each take his censer and put incense in it, and each of you bring his censer before the Lord, two hundred and fifty censers; both you and Aaron, each *with* his censer." So every man took his censer, put fire in it, laid incense on it, and stood at the door of the tabernacle of meeting with Moses and Aaron. And Korah gathered all the congregation against them at the door of the tabernacle of meeting. Then the glory of the Lord appeared to all the congregation.

And the Lord spoke to Moses and Aaron, saying, **"Separate yourselves from among this congregation, that I may consume them in a moment."**

Then they fell on their faces, and said, "**O God, the God of the spirits of all flesh**, shall one man sin, and You be angry with all the congregation?"

So the Lord spoke to Moses, saying, "Speak to the congregation, saying, 'Get away from the tents of Korah, Dathan, and Abiram.' "

Then Moses rose and went to Dathan and Abiram, and the elders of Israel followed him. And he spoke to the congregation, saying, "Depart now from the tents of these wicked men! Touch nothing of theirs, lest you be consumed in all their sins." So they got away from around the tents of Korah, Dathan, and Abiram; and Dathan and Abiram came out and stood at the door of their tents, with their wives, their sons, and their little children.

And Moses said: "By this you shall know that the Lord has sent me to do all these works, for *I have* not *done them* of my own will. If these men die naturally like all men, or if they are visited by the common fate of all men, *then* the Lord has not sent me. But if the Lord creates a new thing, and the earth opens its mouth and swallows them up with all that belongs to them, and they go down alive into the pit, then you will understand that **these men have rejected the Lord**."

Now it came to pass, as he finished speaking all these words, that

the ground split apart under them, and the earth opened its mouth and swallowed them up, with their households and all the men with Korah, with all *their* goods. So they and all those with them went down alive into the pit; the earth closed over them, and they perished from among the assembly. Then all Israel who *were* around them fled at their cry, for they said, "Lest the earth swallow us up *also!*" And a fire came out from the Lord and consumed the two hundred and fifty men who were offering incense.

Then the Lord spoke to Moses, saying: "Tell Eleazar, the son of Aaron the priest, to pick up the censers out of the blaze, for they are holy, and scatter the fire some distance away. The censers of these men who sinned against their own souls, let them be made into hammered plates as a covering for the altar. Because they presented them before the Lord, therefore they are holy; and they shall be a sign to the children of Israel."

So Eleazar the priest took the bronze censers, which those who were burned up had presented, and they were hammered out as a covering on the altar, *to be* a memorial to the children of Israel that no outsider, who *is* not a descendant of Aaron, should come near to offer incense before the Lord, that he might not become like Korah and his companions, just as the Lord had said to him through Moses." **Num. 16:1-40**

"Another scripture comes to me in light of this one: "<u>Touch not My anointed ones and do My prophets no harm</u>." 1 Chr. 16:22

SONS OF ELI

"Now Eli was very old; and **he heard everything his sons did to all Israel, and how they lay with the women who assembled at the door of the tabernacle of meeting**. So he said to them, "Why do you do such things? For I hear of your evil dealings from all the people. No, my sons! For *it is* not a good report that I hear. You make the Lord's people transgress. If one man sins against another, God will judge him. But if a man sins against the Lord, who will intercede for him?" Nevertheless they did not heed the voice of their father, because the Lord desired to kill them.

And the child Samuel grew in stature, and in favor both with the Lord and men.

Then a man of God came to Eli and said to him, "Thus says the Lord: 'Did I not clearly reveal Myself to the house of your father when they were in Egypt in Pharaoh's house? Did I not choose him out of all the tribes of Israel *to be* My priest, to offer upon My altar, to burn incense, and to wear an ephod before Me? And did I not give to the house of your father all the offerings of the children of Israel made by fire? **Why do you kick at My sacrifice and My offering which I have commanded *in My* dwelling place, and honor your sons more than Me, to make yourselves fat with the best of all the offerings of Israel My people?'** Therefore the Lord God of Israel says: 'I said indeed *that* your house and the house of your father would walk before Me forever.' But now the Lord says: 'Far be it from Me; **for those who honor Me I will honor, and those who despise Me shall be lightly esteemed**. Behold, the days are coming that I will cut off your arm and the arm of your father's house, so that there will not be an old man in your house. **And you will see an enemy *in My* dwelling place, *despite* all the good which God does for Israel.** And there shall not be an old man in your house forever. But any of your men *whom* I do not cut off from My altar shall consume your eyes and grieve your heart. And all the descendants of your house shall die in the flower of their age. **Now this *shall be* a sign to you that will come upon your two sons, on Hophni and Phinehas: in one day they shall die, both of them**. Then I will raise up for Myself a **faithful priest** *who* shall do according to what *is* in My heart and in My mind. I will build him a sure house, and he shall walk before My anointed forever. And it shall come to pass that everyone who is left in your house will come *and* bow down to him for a piece of silver and a morsel of bread, and say, "Please, put me in one of the priestly positions, that I may eat a piece of bread."

The Lord clearly reveals His heart once again to sexual defilement and rebellion in His dwelling place of worship and because Eli allowed this, **both sons were destroyed in one day**. Our God is holy and He honors those who honor Him. He is grieved and angry over the sin of dishonor and rebellion.

KING SAUL

Samuel also said to Saul, "The Lord sent me to anoint you king over His people, over Israel. Now therefore, **heed the voice of the words of the Lord**. Thus says the Lord of hosts: **'I will punish Amalek *for* what he did to Israel, how he ambushed him on the way when he came up from Egypt. Now go and**

attack Amalek, and utterly destroy all that they have, and do not spare them. But kill both man and woman, infant and nursing child, ox and sheep, camel and donkey.'" So Saul gathered the people together and numbered them in Telaim, two hundred thousand foot soldiers and ten thousand men of Judah. And Saul came to a city of Amalek, and lay in wait in the valley.

Then Saul said to the Kenites,"Go, depart, get down from among the Amalekites, lest I destroy you with them. For you showed kindness to all the children of Israel when they came up out of Egypt." So the Kenites departed from among the Amalekites. And Saul attacked the Amalekites, from Havilah all the way to Shur, which is east of Egypt. He also took Agag king of the Amalekites alive, and utterly destroyed all the people with the edge of the sword. But Saul and the people spared Agag and the best of the sheep, the oxen, the fatlings, the lambs, and all *that was* good, and were unwilling to utterly destroy them. But everything despised and worthless, that they utterly destroyed.

Now the **word of the Lord** came to Samuel, saying, "I greatly regret that I have set up Saul *as* king, for he has **turned back from following Me, and has not performed My commandments**." And it grieved Samuel, and he cried out to the Lord all night. So when Samuel rose early in the morning to meet Saul, it was told Samuel, saying, "Saul went to Carmel, and indeed, **he set up a monument for himself**; and he has gone on around, passed by, and gone down to Gilgal." Then Samuel went to Saul, and Saul said to him, "Blessed *are* you of the Lord! **I have performed the commandment of the Lord."**

But Samuel said, "What then *is* this bleating of the sheep in my ears, and the lowing of the oxen which I hear?" And Saul said,

"They have brought them from the Amalekites; for the people spared the best of the sheep and the oxen, to sacrifice to the Lord your God; and the rest we have utterly destroyed."

Then Samuel said to Saul, **"Be quiet! And I will tell you what the Lord said to me last night."**

And he said to him, "Speak on." So Samuel said, "When you *were* little in your own eyes, *were* you not head of the tribes of Israel? And did not the Lord anoint you king over Israel? Now the Lord sent you on a mission, and said, 'Go, and utterly destroy the sinners, the Amalekites, and fight against them until they are consumed.' Why then did you **not obey the voice of the Lord?** Why did you swoop down on the spoil, and do evil in the sight of the Lord?"

And Saul said to Samuel, "But I have obeyed the voice of the Lord, and gone on the mission on which the Lord sent me, and brought back Agag king of Amalek; I have utterly destroyed the Amalekites. **But the people took of the plunder, sheep and oxen, the best of the things which should have been utterly destroyed, to sacrifice to the Lord your God in Gilgal."**

So Samuel said: "**Has the Lord *as great* delight in burnt offerings and sacrifices,**
As in obeying the voice of the Lord? Behold, to obey is better than sacrifice,
***And* to heed than the fat of rams. For rebellion *is as* the sin of witchcraft,**
And stubbornness *is as* iniquity and idolatry. Because you have rejected the word of the Lord, He also has rejected you from *being* king."

Then Saul said to Samuel, "I have sinned, for I have transgressed the commandment of the Lord and your words, because **I feared the people and obeyed their voice**. Now therefore, please pardon my sin, and return with me, that I may worship the Lord." But Samuel said to Saul, "I will not return with you, **for you have rejected the word of the Lord, and the Lord has rejected you from being king over Israel."** And as Samuel turned around to go away, *Saul* seized the edge of his robe, and it tore. So Samuel said to him, "The Lord has torn the kingdom of Israel from you today, and has given it to a neighbor of yours, *who is* better than you. And also the Strength of Israel will not lie nor relent. For He *is* not a man, that He should relent."

Then he said, "I have sinned; *yet* honor me now, please, before the elders of my people and before Israel, and return with me, that I may worship the Lord your God." So Samuel turned back after Saul, and Saul worshiped the Lord. Then Samuel said, "Bring Agag king of the Amalekites here to me." So Agag came to him cautiously. And Agag said, "Surely the bitterness of death is past."

But Samuel said, "As your sword has made women childless, so shall your mother be childless among women." And Samuel hacked Agag in pieces before the Lord in Gilgal. Then Samuel went to Ramah, and Saul went up to his house at Gibeah of Saul. And Samuel went no more to see Saul until the day of his death. Nevertheless Samuel mourned for Saul, and the Lord regretted that He had made Saul king over Israel. **1 Sam. 15:1-34**

Saul did what appeared to be a mighty obedient act when he defeated the Amalekites. When I first read this story, I thought, surely he didn't do something too harmful Lord. I highlighted the areas where he disobeyed what the Lord told him to do. He spared the King, let the people take the spoil from the land and **built a monument for himself.** Rebellion and Disobedience cost him his career, his calling and the worst of all, he was rejected by the Lord. Why? He feared the people and obeyed their voice. How many times do we do things like this? I began to search my heart and found many times in my life that I should have obeyed the Lord to say what He said to say or do what He said to do and my own heart has been very convicted!

KING AHAB AND JEZEBEL

King Ahab takes Jezebel as his wife, who is the daughter of King Ethbaal of the Phoenicians. He then went and served Baal and worshiped him by placing an altar for him in the temple and made a 'sacred post.' Jezebel rejects the Lord God of Israel and leads Ahab into accepting her Baal worship. **1 Ki. 16-31-33**

Their sins of rebellion and disobedience to God cost them greatly. The Lord sends Elijah the prophet to confront the 450 prophets of Baal on Mt. Carmel and 400 prophets of Asherah who eat at Jezebel's table. The Lord tries to bring correction by sending Elijah but he is challenged by these Baal worshipers. They danced and pleaded for Baal to appear when Elijah built a wood offering and challenged them to call on Baal to accept the sacrifice. Water was poured on the wood. The fire of God comes down from heaven and consumes the burnt offering when Elijah prayed, and the Lord proved who was truly God! The Lord displays His power before them and Elijah has all the prophets of Baal destroyed. **1 Ki. 18:36-37** After threatening Elijah's life, he escapes to hide from Jezebel. Jehu pursues after Jezebel and she is destroyed by being thrown out a window to her death with dogs eating her. **2Ki. 9:35 OUR GOD WILL NOT BE MOCKED!**

JUDAS ISCARIOT

"Then one of the twelve, called Judas Iscariot, went to the chief priests and said, "What are you willing to give me if I deliver Him to you?" And they counted out to him thirty pieces of silver. So from that time he sought opportunity to betray Him. Now on the first *day of the Feast of the Unleavened Bread* the disciples came to Jesus, saying to Him, "Where do You want us to prepare for You to eat the Passover?" And He said, "Go into the city to a certain man, and say to him, 'The Teacher says, "My time is at hand; I will keep the Passover at your house with My disciples."

So the disciples did as Jesus had directed them; and they prepared the Passover. When evening had come, He sat down with the twelve. Now as they were eating, He said, "**Assuredly, I say to you, one of you will betray Me**." And they were exceedingly sorrowful, and each of them began to say to Him, "Lord, is it I?"

He answered and said, "**He who dipped *his* hand with Me in the dish will betray Me. The Son of Man indeed goes just as it is written of Him, but woe to that man by whom the Son of Man is betrayed! It would have been good for that man if he had not been born.**"

Then Judas, who was betraying Him, answered and said, "Rabbi, is it I?" He said to him, "**You have said it**." **Mat. 26:14**

Judas was one of the twelve chosen disciples who followed Jesus, ate with Him and was taught about the Kingdom; yet, he allowed satan to fill his heart in order to betray Him for thirty pieces of silver. Jesus said you cannot serve God and money. The love of money is the root of all evil. Does that mean God wants you to be poor? No, it is the love of money, honoring money more than the Lord in your heart and serving it all your life instead of Him. Many people spend all their lives pursuing many riches, so that they are labeled as successful and are exalted and famous as a result. Money becomes an idol, carrying away the heart and ruling the lives of the pursuers. You can't take it with you when you die, so many save money all their life to leave it as an inheritance for their loved ones to enjoy and have provision.

"No one can serve two masters; for either he will hate the one and love the other, or else he will be loyal to the one and despise the other. **You cannot serve God and mammon**." **Mat. 6:24**

"A good man leaves an inheritance to his children's children, but the wealth of the sinner is stored up for the righteous." **Pro.13:22**

ANANIAS AND SAPPHIRA

"But a certain man named Ananias, with Sapphira his wife, sold a possession. And he kept back *part* of the proceeds, his wife also being aware *of it,* and brought a certain part and laid *it* at the apostles' feet. But Peter said, "**Ananias, why has Satan filled your heart to lie to the Holy Spirit and keep back *part* of the price of the land for yourself? While it remained, was it not your own? And after it was sold, was it not in your own control? Why have you conceived this thing in your heart? You have not lied to men but to God**."

Then Ananias, hearing these words, fell down and breathed his last. So **great fear came upon all** those who heard these things.

And the young men arose and wrapped him up, carried *him* out, and buried *him.* Now it was about three hours later when his wife came in, not knowing what had happened. And Peter answered her, "Tell me whether you sold the land for so much?" She said, "Yes, for so much."

Then Peter said to her, "How is it that you have **agreed together to <u>test the Spirit of the Lord</u>**? Look, the feet of those who have buried your husband *are* at the door, and they will carry you out." Then immediately she fell down at his feet and breathed her last. And the young men came in and found her dead, and carrying *her* out, buried *her* by her husband. So **<u>great fear came upon all the church and upon all who heard these things</u>." Acts 5:1-11**

There is a great lack of the fear of the Lord in the church today. Many have created a gospel that is incomplete and satisfies their desires, rather than the whole gospel truth which clearly shows the need to be separated from the world and live a holy and Godly life. When the fear of the Lord was released, the church increased in number and brought about an extreme change in their lives.

<u>MY TESTIMONY</u>

For the sake of the revealing of this revelation to current times, I will share a testimony.
Many years ago, I worked for a Christian school as a pre-school teacher and I was so excited about working for this new opportunity where I could share about Jesus freely without losing my job. Every morning, I would read the word and during prayer time, I had a prayer book that I would read out loud and make my Christian confessions over my life and my loved ones, **very religiously.** I would feel so covered with the presence of the Lord for reciting His word over us daily and there was almost a guilt I

would feel if I skipped a day. I know now that was legalism through religious works.

Well one day, I was running late for work and rushed the girls to school and hurried to make it on time. One hour before classes began, the children were dropped off to play. I was assigned to watch over them on the playground to assure their protection. I remembered I hadn't read my prayer book that day and never wanted to miss a day, so I took it out and while looking at the children, began to recite the word in between my glances at them. It took about 20 minutes but when I finished I was so **proud of my great accomplishment** and felt much better.

About an hour after class started, I was called to the Principal's office and asked what I was doing that morning on the playground. I told her I had left in a hurry that morning and brought my prayer book with me as I read it every day. I said I'd read a sentence, then glance at the children.

Thinking that she would commend my efforts as a Christian, her response absolutely shocked me.

"You're Fired." I'm fired? For reading a prayer book at a Christian school? I left so angry that they were so harsh to me over reading God's word.

I shared what happened to my friends at church and they told me, "Diane, rejoice, you have been persecuted for the gospel." Wow, I thought I was sharing in the same suffering that the Apostles experienced. I was so **proud** now to be counted as one of them. I used that incident as a testimony and **belittled that school** for being used of the devil against me; **<u>until</u>** about a week ago while I was studying the word about rebellion.

Here is the truth He shared with me, **"Diane you were not persecuted at that school, you were fired because you rebelled against the authority of the school and disobeyed their rules and the reason they hired you. You have <u>judged them</u> and <u>exalted yourself</u>. Repent." "<u>Judge not</u>, that you be**

not judged. For with what judgment you judge, you will be judged; and with the measure you use, it will be measured back to you. And why do you look at the speck in your brother's eye, but do not consider the plank in your own eye? Or how can you say to your brother, 'Let me remove the speck from your eye'; and look, a plank *is* in your own eye? Hypocrite! First remove the plank from your own eye, and then you will see clearly to remove the speck from your brother's eye." Mat. 7:1-5
This is where **religious works** can cause a self-exaltation to come secretly in our hearts if we are not careful. When this sin enters in, you begin to pride yourself as better than most other believers and more loved by God than those lousy sinners out there. We must live and walk humbly before our God **daily.** He is the one who is to be **exalted, praised, worshiped and thanked** for all He has done for us through His **death, burial and resurrection**. Forgive us Lord and please help us all to stay humble before You always and to be daily demonstrators of Your love to **all others**.

Father, forgive me for the times that I judged others for things they never did. Forgive me for the pointed finger I've used against any person. Help me to "get all the facts of the matter" before I proceed to judge someone else.
You have been so merciful to forgive me of my sins when I ask You. Help me to be just as merciful toward others I pray in Jesus' Mighty Name, amen.

CHAPTER 4
WHAT IS OBEDIENCE?

The definition for the word obedience is: compliance with an order, request, or law or submission to another's authority; an act or instance of obeying. There are several incredible examples of obedience in the scriptures written for us to see how important this for our lives. Obedience is a choice, not a force. The fruit that is produced from the result of obeying God's voice could determine our future blessing or curse, life or death. We should always choose life!
Let's begin with Noah.

<u>NOAH</u>

"This is the genealogy of Noah. Noah was a **just man**, perfect in his generations. Noah **walked with God**. And Noah begot three sons: Shem, Ham, and Japheth. The earth also was corrupt before God, and the earth was filled with violence. So God looked upon the earth, and indeed it was corrupt; for all flesh had corrupted their way on the earth.

THE ARK PREPARED

And God said to Noah, "The **end of all flesh has come before Me**, for the earth is <u>filled with violence</u> through them; and behold, **I will destroy them with the earth**. Make yourself an ark of gopher wood; make rooms in the ark, and cover it inside and outside with pitch. And this is how you shall make it: The length of the ark *shall be* three hundred cubits, its width fifty cubits, and its height thirty cubits. You shall make a window for the ark, and you shall finish it to a cubit from above; and set the door of the ark in its side.

You shall make it *with* lower, second, and third *decks.* And behold, I Myself am bringing floodwaters on the earth, to destroy from under heaven all flesh in which *is* the breath of life; everything that *is* on the earth shall die. But I will establish My covenant with you; and you shall go into the ark—you, your sons, your wife, and your sons' wives with you. And of every living thing of all flesh you shall bring two of every *sort* into the ark, to keep *them* alive with you; they shall be male and female. Of the birds after their kind, of animals after their kind, and of every creeping thing of the earth after its kind, two of every *kind* will come to you to keep *them* alive. And you shall take for yourself of all food that is eaten, and you shall gather *it* to yourself; and it shall be food for you and for them." **Thus Noah did; according to all that God commanded him, so he did**." **Gen. 6:1-22**

The Lord spared Noah and his seed because he was a just man who pleased the Lord and **obeyed His voice**. In the natural, it looked ridiculous to build a huge ship on dry land and fill it with animals, but the results were devastating for those who were left behind because of the sin of **violence, rebellion and disobedience**.

ABRAHAM

One of my favorite examples of obedience is with Abraham and his son of promise, Isaac.
"Now it came to pass after these things that God tested Abraham, and said to him, "Abraham!" And he said, "Here I am." Then He said, **"Take now your son, your only *son* Isaac, whom you love, and go to the land of Moriah, and offer him there as a burnt**

offering on one of the mountains of which I shall tell you." So Abraham rose early in the morning and saddled his donkey, and took two of his young men with him, and Isaac his son; and he split the wood for the burnt offering, and arose and went to the place of which God had told him.

Then on the third day Abraham lifted his eyes and saw the place afar off. And Abraham said to his young men, "Stay here with the donkey; the lad and I will go yonder and worship, and we will come back to you."

So Abraham took the wood of the burnt offering and laid *it* on Isaac his son; and he took the fire in his hand, and a knife, and the two of them went together. But Isaac spoke to Abraham his father and said, "My father!" And he said, "Here I am, my son." Then he said, "Look, the fire and the wood, but where *is* the lamb for a burnt offering?" And Abraham said, **"My son, God will provide for Himself the lamb for a burnt offering."** So the two of them went together.

Then they came to the place of which **God had told him**. And Abraham built an altar there and placed the wood in order; and he bound Isaac his son and laid him on the altar, upon the wood. And Abraham stretched out his hand and took the knife to slay his son. But the Angel of the Lord called to him from heaven and said, "Abraham, Abraham!" So he said, "Here I am."

And He said, "**Do not lay your hand on the lad, or do anything to him; for now I know that you fear God, since you have not withheld your son, your only *son,* from Me.**" Then Abraham lifted his eyes and looked, and there behind *him was* a ram caught in a thicket by its horns. So Abraham went and took the ram, and offered it up for a burnt offering instead of his son. And Abraham called the name of the place, The-Lord-Will-Provide; as it is said *to* this day, **"In the <u>Mount of the Lord</u> it shall be provided."**

Then the Angel of the Lord called to Abraham a second time out of heaven, and said: **"By Myself I have sworn, says the Lord, because you have done this thing, and have not withheld your son, your only *son;* blessing** I will bless you, and **multiplying** I will multiply your descendants as the stars of the heaven and as the sand which *is* on the seashore; and **<u>your descendants shall possess the gate of their enemies. In your seed all the nations of the earth shall be blessed, because you have obeyed My voice</u>." Gen. 22:1-18**

Every time I've read that story, I put myself in the place of Abraham and question myself: Would I ever obey like he did? Praise God, he didn't have to go through with it, but praise God, he feared God, obeyed His word and passed the test of obedience! I can't wait to thank him when I meet him one day in heaven.

<u>MOSES</u>

Now Moses was tending the flock of Jethro his father-in-law, the priest of Midian. And he led the flock to the back of the desert, and came to Horeb, the mountain of God. And the Angel of the Lord appeared to him in a flame of fire from the midst of a bush. So he looked, and behold, the bush was burning with fire, but the bush *was* not consumed. Then Moses said, "I will now turn aside and see this great sight, why the bush does not burn."

So when the Lord saw that he turned aside to look, God called to him from the midst of the bush and said, **"Moses, Moses!"** And he said, "Here I am."

Then He said, **"Do not draw near this place. Take your sandals off your feet, for the place where you stand *is* holy ground."** Moreover He said, **"I *am* the God of your father—the God of Abraham, the God of Isaac, and the God of Jacob."** And Moses hid his face, for he was afraid to look upon God. And the Lord said: **"I have surely seen the oppression of My people who *are* in Egypt, and have heard their cry because of their taskmasters, for I know their sorrows. So I have come down to deliver them out of the hand of the Egyptians, and to bring them up from that land to a good and large land, to a land flowing with milk and honey, to the place of the Canaanites and the Hittites and the Amorites and the Perizzites and the Hivites and the Jebusites. Now therefore, behold, the cry of the children of Israel has come to Me, and I have also seen the oppression with which the Egyptians oppress them. Come now, therefore, and I will send you to Pharaoh that you may bring My people, the children of Israel, out of Egypt."**

But Moses said to God, "Who *am* I that I should go to Pharaoh, and that I should bring the children of Israel out of Egypt?"

So He said, **"I will certainly be with you. And this *shall be* a sign to you that I have sent you: When you have brought the people out of Egypt, you shall <u>serve God on this mountain</u>."**

Then Moses said to God, "Indeed, *when* I come to the children of Israel and say to them, 'The God of your fathers has sent me to you,' and they say to me, 'What *is* His name?' what shall I say to them?"

And God said to Moses, "**I AM WHO I AM.**" And He said, **"Thus you shall say to the children of Israel, "I AM" has sent me to you.' "** Moreover God said to Moses, "**Thus you shall say to the children of Israel: 'The Lord God of your fathers, the God of Abraham, the God of Isaac, and the God of Jacob, has sent me to you. This *is* My name forever, and this *is* My memorial to all generations.' Go and gather the elders of Israel together, and say to them, 'The Lord God of your fathers, the God of Abraham, of Isaac, and of Jacob, appeared to me, saying, "I have surely visited you and *seen* what is done to you in Egypt; and I have said I will bring you up out of the affliction of Egypt to the land of the Canaanites and the Hittites and the Amorites and the Perizzites and the Hivites and the Jebusites, to a land flowing with milk and honey.' Then they will heed your voice; and you shall come, you and the elders of Israel, to the king of Egypt; and you shall say to him, 'The Lord God of the Hebrews has met with us; and now, please, let us go three days' journey into the wilderness, that we may sacrifice to the Lord our God.' But I am sure that the king of Egypt will not let you go, no, not even by a mighty hand. So I will stretch out My hand and strike Egypt with all My wonders which I will do in its midst; and after that he will let you go. And I will give this people favor in the sight of the Egyptians; and it shall be, when you go, that you shall not go empty-handed. But every woman shall ask of her neighbor, namely, of her who dwells near her house, articles of silver, articles of gold, and clothing; and you shall put *them* on your**

sons and on your daughters. So you shall plunder the Egyptians." Ex. 3:1-22

Moses' life was an extraordinary one. He was led up the mountain of God to meet with Him face to face. His chosen people were in bondage in Egypt and the Lord wanted them free. He needed a mouthpiece to speak through and Moses was His choice, but he became extremely resistant as he stuttered in his speech and didn't feel qualified to be used. "So the anger of the Lord was kindled against Moses, and He said: "**Is not Aaron the Levite your brother? I know that he can speak well. And look, he is also coming out to meet you. When he sees you, he will be glad in his heart." Exodus 4:14**

His rebellion and disobedience produced the anger of the Lord. After they were freed from Egypt, they became rebellious and began sinning against the Lord. His commandments were then released to them.

"And Moses called all Israel, and said to them: "Hear, O Israel, the statutes and judgments which I speak in your hearing today, that you may **learn them and be careful to observe them**. The Lord our God made a covenant with us in Horeb. The Lord did not make this covenant with our fathers, but with us, those who *are* here today, all of us who *are* alive. The Lord talked with you face to face on the mountain from the midst of the fire. I stood between the Lord and you at that time, to declare to you the word of the Lord; for you were afraid because of the fire, and you did not go up the mountain.

He said: **'I *am* the Lord your God who brought you out of the land of Egypt, out of the house of bondage.**

'You shall have no other gods before Me.
'You shall not make for yourself a carved image—any likeness *of anything* that *is* in heaven above, or that *is* in the earth beneath, or that *is* in the water under the earth; you shall not bow down to them nor serve them. For I, the Lord your God, *am* a jealous God, visiting the iniquity of the fathers upon the children to the third and fourth *generations* of those who hate Me, but showing mercy to thousands, to those who love Me and keep My commandments.
'You shall not take the name of the Lord your God in vain, for the Lord will not hold *him* guiltless who takes His name in vain.
'Observe the Sabbath day, to keep it holy, as the Lord your God commanded you.
Six days you shall labor and do all your work, but the seventh day *is* the Sabbath of the Lord your God. *In it* you shall do no work: you, nor your son, nor your daughter, nor your male servant, nor your female servant, nor your ox, nor your donkey, nor any of your cattle, nor your stranger who *is* within your gates, that your male servant and your female servant may rest as well as you. And remember that you were a slave in the land of Egypt, and the Lord your God brought you out from there by a mighty hand and by an outstretched arm; therefore the Lord your God commanded you to keep the Sabbath day.

'Honor your father and your mother, as the Lord your God has commanded you, that your days may be long, and that it may be well with you in the land which the Lord your God is giving you.
'You shall not murder.
'You shall not commit adultery.
'You shall not steal.
'You shall not bear false witness against your neighbor.
'You shall not covet your neighbor's wife; and you shall not desire your neighbor's house, his field, his male servant, his female servant, his ox, his donkey, or anything that *is* your neighbor's.
"These words the Lord spoke to all your assembly, in the mountain from the midst of the fire, the cloud, and the thick darkness, with a loud voice; and He added no more. And He wrote them on two tablets of stone and gave them to me."
Deut. 5:1-22

None of mankind could keep the whole law. It was released to us to show the need for a Savior. Thank You Lord for Your mercy toward mankind in sending us the eternal help we needed in the person of Jesus Christ. We are forever grateful to You.

CHAPTER 5

THE TRADITIONS OF MAN

The Lord shows the response of His heart regarding the actions of His creation. The first commandment is regarding "**no other Gods**" placed before Him and His jealousy over anything or anyone taking that place in our hearts. I began to think of the multiple Gods that have been worshiped in this earth through various religions.

SANTA CLAUS

I thought about "Santa Claus" replacing the role of the true Christmas celebration. Is it not supposed to be about Jesus Christ entering this world to redeem mankind from sin? The commercial world spends billions of dollars each year advertising Santa products, food, lights and the best gifts of every sort for each other and setting up a tree to decorate. The malls are jammed with Santa and millions of children getting the opportunity to sit on his lap. We have made this practice a "**yearly tradition**" in our lives. I've read real life stories of how people have trampled over one another in stores, just so they could buy their child that favorite Christmas gift on the market that is sold at a discount price. It's all about us, not Him.

I decided to look up online where these very famous traditions originated from. Here is what I found: The **legend** of Santa Claus can be traced back hundreds of years to a monk named St. Nicholas. It is believed that Nicholas was born sometime around 280 A.D. in Patara, near Myra in modern day Turkey. Much admired for his piety and kindness, St. Nicholas became the subject of **many legends**. Legend defined: A traditional story sometimes popularly regarded as historical, but unauthenticated. Please look this information up yourself online.

EASTER

Then the celebration of the resurrection of Christ, we call it Easter. This is another **"yearly tradition"** that was formed to replace or "add to" the fun of the season. It was very popular with the Catholics. We entertain our children with the stories about the Easter Bunny and color eggs, hunt them and eat our candy as the reward. The church has displayed the fun and excitement over these "seemingly innocent" seasons. The true reason for the Resurrection Day Celebration is Christ dying for the sins of mankind and rising from the tomb as He conquered death, hell and the grave. He competes with the Easter Bunny and all the fun and our children are all following the God of entertainment every year.

As I looked up the origin of Easter online, here is what I found: "The naming of the celebration as "Easter" seems to go back to the name of a pre-Christian goddess in England, Eostre, who was celebrated at beginning of Spring. The only reference to this goddess comes from the writings of the Verable Bede, a British monk who lived in the late seventh and early eighth century." It was approved by Emperor Constantine, who favored Christianity in A.D. 325. It was decided that Easter should be fixed on the first Sunday after the first full moon of the vernal equinox. The German immigrants settled in Pennsylvania in the 18th and 19th century and brought this tradition with them to the U.S. Please look this up online for further information.

HALLOWEEN

The next famous ceremony I need to share with you is another yearly celebration held on October 31st called Halloween. It originated with the Ancient Celtic festival of Samhain, when people would light bonfires and wear costumes to ward off ghosts. The Celts who lived 2000 years ago in the area that is now Ireland, The United Kingdom and northern France, celebrated their new year on November 1. The day marked the end of the summer and the harvest and the beginning of the dark, cold winter, a time of year that was often associated with human death. Celts believed that on the night before the new year, the boundary between the worlds of the living and the dead became blurred. On the night of October 31 they celebrated Samhain, when it was believed that ghosts of the dead returned to earth. In addition to causing trouble and damaging crops, Celts thought that the presence of the otherworldly spirits made it easier for the Druids, or Celtic Priests, to make predictions about the future. To commemorate the event, Druids built huge sacred bonfires, where the people gathered to burn crops and animals as sacrifices to the Celtic deities. During the celebration the Celts wore costumes, typically consisting of animal heads and skins, and attempted to tell each other's fortunes.

In the eighth century, Pope Gregory III designated November 1 as a time to honor all saints; soon, All Saints Day incorporated some of the traditions of Samhain. The evening before was known as All Hallows Eve, and later Halloween. Over time, Halloween evolved into a day of activities like trick-or-treating, carving jack-o-lanterns, festive gatherings, donning costumes and eating sweet treats. This tradition continues annually and again, billions of dollars flood the stores in order to purchase the sweet treats and costumes. You can read up more on these subjects online. Now that these events are explained, the question is this: Do you think the Lord is pleased with these traditions being a part of a Christian family's life? I have heard testimonies from former witches and warlocks who have exposed these satanic practices on Youtube as well as in person. Two names to look up would be Carol Kornacki and John Ramirez. Both of these powerful testimonies expose the origin and practice of witchcraft, coming from former participants in the craft. What bothers me the most for anyone involved in these traditions is the spiritual price tag attached to them. Please pray and ask the Lord what He would have you to do. Always remember, the choice is yours.

The scriptures that come to me to share with you are:

"Therefore, putting away lying, "Let each one of you speak truth with his neighbor," for we are members of one another. "Be angry, and do not sin": do not let the sun go down on your wrath, **nor give place to the devil. Let him who stole steal no longer,** but rather let him labor, working with his hands what is good, that he may have something to give him who has need. Let no corrupt word proceed out of your mouth, but what is good for necessary edification, that it may impart grace to the hearers. And do not grieve the Holy Spirit of God, by whom you were sealed for the day of redemption. Let all bitterness, wrath, anger, clamor, and evil speaking be put away from you, with all malice. And be kind to one another, tenderhearted, forgiving one another, even as God in Christ forgave you." **Ephes. 4:25-32**

"My people are destroyed for lack of knowledge. Because you have rejected knowledge, I also will reject you from being priest for Me; Because you have forgotten the law of your God, I also will forget your children." **Hos. 4:6**

"He who believes in Him is not condemned; but he who does not believe is condemned already, because he has not believed in the name of the only begotten Son of God. And **this is the condemnation, that the light has come into the world, and men loved darkness rather than light, because their deeds were evil. For everyone practicing evil hates the light and does not come to the light, lest his deeds should be exposed. But he who does the truth comes to the light, that his deeds may be clearly seen, that they have been done in God**." **Jn. 3:18-21**

"Do not be unequally yoked together with unbelievers. For what fellowship has righteousness with lawlessness? **And what communion has light with darkness?** And what **accord has Christ with Belial?** Or what part has a believer with an unbeliever? And **what agreement has the temple of God with idols?** For you are the temple of the living God. As God has said: "I will dwell in them and walk among *them.* I will be their God, and they shall be My people." Therefore, "Come out from among them and **be separate, says the Lord. Do not touch what is unclean,**

and I will receive you." "I will be a Father to you, And you shall be **My sons and daughters**, Says the Lord Almighty." **2 Cor. 6:14-18**

The assignment given to Moses was to lead the Israelites into the promised land the Lord had prepared for them. It was a land flowing with milk and honey. Moses was instructed to do something but disobedience arose and it caused a huge hindrance for him and the people.

"Then the children of Israel, the whole congregation, came into the Wilderness of Zin in the first month, and the people stayed in Kadesh; and Miriam died there and was buried there. Now there was **no water** for the congregation; so they gathered together against Moses and Aaron. And the people contended with Moses and spoke, saying: "If only we had died when our brethren died before the Lord! Why have you brought up the assembly of the Lord into this wilderness, that we and our animals should die here? And why have you made us come up out of Egypt, to bring us to this evil place? It *is* not a place of grain or figs or vines or pomegranates; nor *is* there any water to drink." So Moses and Aaron went from the presence of the assembly to the door of the tabernacle of meeting, and <u>they fell on their faces</u>. And **the glory of the Lord <u>appeared to them</u>.**

Then the Lord spoke to Moses, saying, "**Take the rod; you and your brother Aaron gather the congregation together. <u>Speak to the rock</u> before their eyes, and it will yield its water; thus you shall bring water for them out of the rock, and give drink to the congregation and their animals."** So Moses took the rod from before the Lord **as He commanded him**.

And Moses and Aaron gathered the assembly together before the rock; and he said to them, "Hear now, you **rebels**! Must **we** bring water for you out of this rock?" Then Moses lifted his hand and **struck the rock twice with his rod**; and water came out abundantly, and the congregation and their animals drank.

Then the Lord spoke to Moses and Aaron, "**Because you did not believe Me, to hallow Me in the eyes of the children of Israel, therefore you shall not bring this assembly into the land which I have given them**." **Num. 20:1-13**

Rebellion and disobedience cost Moses the greatest finish to his calling and he wasn't able to enter the promised land. How sad when we disobey, I'm sure he regretted his choice, but it was his choice to obey or disobey.

KING DAVID

Now the Lord said to Samuel, **"How long will you mourn for Saul, seeing I have rejected him from reigning over Israel? Fill your horn with oil, and go; I am sending you to Jesse the Bethlehemite. For I have provided Myself a king among his sons."**

And Samuel said, "How can I go? If Saul hears *it,* he will kill me."

But the Lord said, **"Take a heifer with you, and say, 'I have come to sacrifice to the Lord.' Then invite Jesse to the sacrifice, and I will show you what you shall do; you shall anoint for Me the one I name to you."**

So Samuel did what the Lord said, and went to Bethlehem. And the elders of the town trembled at his coming, and said, "Do you come peaceably?"

And he said, "Peaceably; I have come to sacrifice to the Lord. Sanctify yourselves, and come with me to the sacrifice." Then he consecrated Jesse and his sons, and invited them to the sacrifice.

So it was, when they came, that he looked at Eliab and said, "Surely the Lord's anointed *is* before Him!"

But the Lord said to Samuel, "**Do not look at his appearance or at his physical stature, because I have refused him. For *the Lord does* not *see* as man sees; for <u>man looks at the outward appearance, but the Lord looks at the heart."</u>**

So Jesse called Abinadab, and made him pass before Samuel. And he said, "Neither has the Lord chosen this one." Then Jesse made Shammah pass by. And he said, "Neither has the Lord chosen this one." Thus Jesse made seven of his sons pass before Samuel. And Samuel said to Jesse, "The Lord has not chosen these." And Samuel said to Jesse, "Are all the young men here?" Then he said, "There remains yet the youngest, and there he is, keeping the sheep."

And Samuel said to Jesse, "Send and bring him. For we will not sit down till he comes here." So he sent and brought him in. Now he *was* ruddy, with bright eyes, and good-looking. And the Lord said, "Arise, anoint him; for this *is* the one!" Then Samuel took the horn of oil and anointed him in the midst of his brothers; and the Spirit of the Lord came upon David from that day forward." **1**

Sam. 16:1-16

DAVID AND BATHSHEBA

"It happened in the spring of the year, at the time when kings go out *to battle,* that David sent Joab and his servants with him, and all Israel; and they destroyed the people of Ammon and besieged Rabbah. But David remained at Jerusalem. Then it happened one evening that David arose from his bed and walked on the roof of the king's house. And from the roof **he saw a woman bathing, and the woman *was* very beautiful to behold**. So David sent and inquired about the woman. And *someone* said, "*Is* this not Bathsheba, the daughter of Eliam, the wife of Uriah the Hittite?" Then David sent messengers, and took her; and she came to him, and he lay with her, for she was cleansed from her impurity; and she returned to her house. And the woman conceived; so she sent and told David, and said, "I *am* with child."

Then David sent to Joab, *saying,* "Send me Uriah the Hittite." And Joab sent Uriah to David. When Uriah had come to him, David asked how Joab was doing, and how the people were doing, and how the war prospered. And David said to Uriah, "Go down to your house and wash your feet." So Uriah departed from the king's house, and a gift of food from the king followed him. But Uriah slept at the door of the king's house with all the servants of his lord, and did not go down to his house. So when they told David, saying, "Uriah did not go down to his house," David said to Uriah, "Did you not come from a journey? Why did you not go down to your house?"

And Uriah said to David, "The ark and Israel and Judah are

dwelling in tents, and my lord Joab and the servants of my lord are encamped in the open fields. Shall I then go to my house to eat and drink, and to lie with my wife? *As* you live, and *as* your soul lives, I will not do this thing."

Then David said to Uriah, "Wait here today also, and tomorrow I will let you depart." So Uriah remained in Jerusalem that day and the next. Now when David called him, he ate and drank before him; and he made him drunk. And at evening he went out to lie on his bed with the servants of his lord, but he did not go down to his house.

In the morning it happened that David wrote a letter to Joab and sent *it* by the hand of Uriah. And he wrote in the letter, saying, "Set Uriah in the forefront of the hottest battle, and retreat from him, that he may be struck down and die." So it was, while Joab besieged the city, that he assigned Uriah to a place where he knew there *were* valiant men. Then the men of the city came out and fought with Joab. And *some* of the people of the servants of David fell; and Uriah the Hittite died also.

Then Joab sent and told David all the things concerning the war, and charged the messenger, saying, "When you have finished telling the matters of the war to the king, if it happens that the king's wrath rises, and he says to you: 'Why did you approach so near to the city when you fought? Did you not know that they would shoot from the wall? Who struck Abimelech the son of Jerubbesheth? Was it not a woman who cast a piece of a millstone on him from the wall, so that he died in Thebez? Why did you go near the wall?'—then you shall say, 'Your servant

Uriah the Hittite is dead also.' "

So the messenger went, and came and told David all that Joab had sent by him. And the messenger said to David, "Surely the men prevailed against us and came out to us in the field; then we drove them back as far as the entrance of the gate. The archers shot from the wall at your servants; and *some* of the king's servants are dead, and your servant Uriah the Hittite is dead also."

Then David said to the messenger, "Thus you shall say to Joab: 'Do not let this thing displease you, for the sword devours one as well as another. Strengthen your attack against the city, and overthrow it.' So encourage him."

When the wife of Uriah heard that Uriah her husband was dead, she mourned for her husband. And when her mourning was over, David sent and brought her to his house, and she became his wife and bore him a son. **But the thing that David had done displeased the Lord."**

Then the Lord sent Nathan to David. And he came to him, and said to him: "There were two men in one city, one rich and the other poor. The rich *man* had exceedingly many flocks and herds. But the poor *man* had nothing, except one little ewe lamb which he had bought and nourished; and it grew up together with him and with his children. It ate of his own food and drank from his own cup and lay in his bosom; and it was like a daughter to him. And a traveler came to the rich man, who refused to take from his own flock and from his own herd to prepare one for the wayfaring man who had come to him; but he took the poor man's lamb and prepared it for the man who had come to him."

So David's anger was greatly aroused against the man, and he said to Nathan, "*As* the Lord lives, the man who has done this shall surely die! And he shall restore fourfold for the lamb, because he did this thing and because he had no pity."

Then Nathan said to David, **"You *are* the man!** Thus says the Lord God of Israel: 'I anointed you king over Israel, and I delivered you from the hand of Saul. I gave you your master's house and your master's wives into your keeping, and gave you the house of Israel and Judah. And if *that had been* too little, I also would have given you much more! **Why have you despised the commandment of the Lord, to do evil in His sight? You have killed Uriah the Hittite with the sword; you have taken his wife *to be* your wife, and have killed him with the sword of the people of Ammon. Now therefore, the sword shall never depart from your house, because you have despised Me, and have taken the wife of Uriah the Hittite to be your wife**.' Thus says the Lord: 'Behold, **I will raise up adversity against you from your own house; and I will take your wives before your eyes and give *them* to your neighbor, and he shall lie with your wives in the sight of this sun. For you did *it* secretly, but I will do this thing before all Israel, before the sun.' "**

So David said to Nathan, "**I have sinned against the Lord**."

And Nathan said to David, "**The Lord also has put away your sin; you shall not die**. **However**, because by this deed you have given great occasion to the enemies of the Lord to blaspheme, **the child also who is born to you shall surely die**." Then Nathan departed to his house."

And the Lord struck the child that Uriah's wife bore to David, and it became ill. David therefore pleaded with God for the child, and David fasted and went in and lay all night on the ground. So the elders of his house arose *and went* to him, to raise him up from the ground. But he would not, nor did he eat food with them. Then on the seventh day **it came to pass that the child died**. And the servants of David were afraid to tell him that the child was dead. For they said, "Indeed, while the child was alive, we spoke to him, and he would not heed our voice. How can we tell him that the child is dead? He may do some harm!"

When David saw that his servants were whispering, David perceived that the child was dead. Therefore David said to his servants, "Is the child dead?" And they said, "He is dead."

So David arose from the ground, washed and anointed himself, and changed his clothes; and he went into the house of the Lord and worshiped. Then he went to his own house; and when he requested, they set food before him, and he ate. Then his servants said to him, "What *is* this that you have done? You fasted and wept for the child *while he was* alive, but when the child died, you arose and ate food."

And he said, "While the child was alive, I fasted and wept; for I said, 'Who can tell *whether* the Lord will be gracious to me, that the child may live?' But now he is dead; why should I fast? Can I bring him back again? I shall go to him, but he shall not return to me." **2 Sam. 12:1-23**

David surely saw the consequences for the sin of adultery as it cost him his son who he loved, even though he fasted in prayer and repented before the Lord. **The word of the Lord comes to pass**. The disobedience was sin and the Lord would not hear David's prayers. "If I regard iniquity in my heart, the Lord will not hear." **Ps. 66:18**

David had a heart of repentance and the Lord forgave him of his sin. He had a heart that worshiped the Lord also and the Lord loves those who worship Him in spirit and in truth.

"But the hour is coming and now is. when the true worshipers will worship the Father in spirit and truth; for the Father is seeking such to worship Him." Jn. 4:23

JOB (FEARED GOD)

There was a man in the land of Uz, whose name *was* Job; and that man was **blameless and upright, and one who feared God and shunned evil**. And seven sons and three daughters were born to him. Also, his possessions were seven thousand sheep, three thousand camels, five hundred yoke of oxen, five hundred female donkeys, and a very large household, so that **this man was the greatest of all the people of the East**.

And his sons would go and feast *in their* houses, each on his *appointed* day, and would send and invite their three sisters to eat and drink with them. So it was, when the days of feasting had run their course, that Job would send and **sanctify them**, and he would **rise early in the morning and offer burnt offerings *according to* the number of them all. For Job said, "It may be that my sons have sinned and cursed God in their hearts." Thus Job did regularly.**

Now there was a day when the sons of God came to present themselves before the Lord, and Satan also came among them. And the Lord said to Satan, "From where do you come?"

So Satan answered the Lord and said, "From going to and fro on the earth, and from walking back and forth on it."

Then the Lord said to Satan, "Have you considered My servant Job, that *there is* **none like him on the earth, a blameless and upright man, one who fears God and shuns evil?"**

So Satan answered the Lord and said, **"Does Job fear God for nothing? Have You not made a hedge around him, around his household, and around all that he has on every side? You have blessed the work of his hands, and his possessions have increased in the land. But now,**

stretch out Your hand and touch all that he has, and he will surely curse You to Your face!"

And the Lord said to Satan, **"Behold, all that he has *is* in your power; only do not lay a hand on his *person.*"** So Satan went out from the presence of the Lord.

Now there was a day when his sons and daughters *were* eating and drinking wine in their oldest brother's house; and a messenger came to Job and said, "The oxen were plowing and the donkeys feeding beside them, when the Sabeans raided *them* and took them away—indeed they have killed the servants with the edge of the sword; and I alone have escaped to tell you!"

While he *was* still speaking, another also came and said, "The fire of God fell from heaven and burned up the sheep and the servants, and consumed them; and I alone have escaped to tell you!"

While he *was* still speaking, another also came and said, "The Chaldeans formed three bands, raided the camels and took them away, yes, and killed the servants with the edge of the sword; and I alone have escaped to tell you!"

While he *was* still speaking, another also came and said, "Your sons and daughters *were* eating and drinking wine in their oldest brother's house, and **suddenly a great wind came from across the wilderness and struck the four corners of the house, and it fell on the young people, and they are dead**; and I alone have escaped to tell you!"

Then Job arose, tore his robe, and shaved his head; and **he fell to the ground and worshiped**. And he said: **"Naked I came from my mother's womb, And naked shall I return there.**
The Lord gave, and the Lord has taken away; Blessed be the name of the Lord." In all this Job did not sin nor charge God with wrong.

Job was hit with one of the harshest obedience tests of all, except for Jesus. Imagine being the richest man in the city and having a family; then all of a sudden you lose them all, including your health, provision and family. What would you do? Job fell to the ground and worshiped the Lord. This man knew the Lord and lived a sanctified life before Him. He had every blessing in life and in one day, lost it all. His wife wanted him to curse God and die. His loyalty and obedience to the Lord paid off later when he prayed for his friends, who accused him of sinning against the

Lord. Job's obedience caused the Lord to restore **double** back to him as a result in every area of loss. This man had a relationship with God and knew His ways.

JOHN THE BAPTIST (PROPHET)

"At that time Herod the tetrarch heard the report about Jesus and said to his servants, "This is John the Baptist; he is risen from the dead, and therefore these powers are at work in him." For Herod had laid hold of John and bound him, and put *him* in prison for the sake of Herodias, his brother Philip's wife. Because John had said to him, **"It is not lawful for you to have her."** And although he wanted to put him to death, he feared the multitude, because they counted him as a prophet.

But when Herod's birthday was celebrated, the daughter of Herodias danced before them and pleased Herod. Therefore he promised with an oath to give her whatever she might ask. So she, having been prompted by her mother, said, "Give me John the Baptist's head here on a platter." And the king was sorry; nevertheless, because of the oaths and because of those who sat with him, he commanded *it* to be given to *her.* So he sent and had John beheaded in prison. And his head was brought on a platter and given to the girl, and she brought *it* to her mother. Then his disciples came and took away the body and buried it, and went and told Jesus." **Mat. 14:1-12**

John the Baptist, the first martyr recorded in the New Testament, was a man who feared God more than any man, even Governmental leaders who lived in rebellion and disobedience knew his undeniable faith and obedience to God. John was fearless, never hesitated to speak the truth regarding sin and he led those who listened, into a baptism of repentance. He operated in such a bold prophetic anointing that it shook the hearts of the leaders and many of the people were afraid of him. The true prophetic word will **reveal the secrets of your heart**, so you will **know** that only God knew these things about you. What God reveals, He desires to heal. The devil hates the prophet because he speaks out God's words of correction to uproot the sin and sows the word of truth to bring freedom and deliverance. Satan is a liar and the father of lies, and the prophetic word of the Lord exposes his lies. The enemy cannot predict your future, only God can.

PETER

"And the Lord said, "Simon, Simon! Indeed Satan has asked for you, that he may sift you as wheat. But I have prayed for you, that your faith should not fail; and when you have returned to Me, strengthen your brethren." But he said to Him, "Lord, I am ready to go with you, both to prison and to death." Then He said, "I tell you Peter, the rooster shall not crow this day before you will **deny three times that you know Me.**" **Luke 22:31-34**

Peter denied knowing Jesus because he feared for his life. Jesus knew this would happen and released a word of wisdom to him that came to pass.

PAUL (APOSTLE)

"Then Paul stood up, and motioning with *his* hand said, "Men of Israel, and you who **fear God,** listen: The God of this people Israel chose our fathers, and exalted the people when they dwelt as strangers in the land of Egypt, and with an uplifted arm He brought them out of it. Now for a time of about **<u>forty years He put up with their ways in the wilderness</u>**. And when He had destroyed seven nations in the land of Canaan, He distributed their land to them by allotment.

"After that He gave *them* judges for about four hundred and fifty years, until Samuel the prophet. And afterward they asked for a king; so God gave them Saul the son of Kish, a man of the tribe of Benjamin, for forty years. And when He had removed him, He raised up for them David as king, to whom also He gave testimony and said, **'I have found David the *son* of Jesse, a man <u>after My *own* heart</u>, who will do all My will.'**

From this man's seed, according to *the* promise, God raised up for Israel Savior—Jesus—after John had first preached, before His coming, the baptism of repentance to all the people of Israel. And as John was finishing his course, he said, 'Who do you think I am? I am not *He.* But behold, there comes One after me, the sandals of whose feet I am not worthy to loose.' "**Men *and* brethren, sons of the family of Abraham, and those among you who fear God, to you the word of this salvation has been sent**. For those who dwell in Jerusalem, and their rulers, because they did not know Him, nor even the voices of the Prophets which are read every Sabbath, have fulfilled *them* in condemning *Him.* And though they found no cause for death *in Him,* they asked Pilate that He should be put to death. Now when they had fulfilled all that was written concerning Him, they took *Him* down from the tree and laid *Him* in a tomb. But God raised Him from the dead. He was seen for many days by those who came up with

Him from Galilee to Jerusalem, who are His witnesses to the people. And we declare to you glad tidings—that promise which was made to the fathers. God has fulfilled this for us their children, in that He has raised up Jesus. As it is also written in the second Psalm: 'You are My Son, Today I have begotten You.' And that He raised Him from the dead, no more to return to corruption, He has spoken thus: **'I will give you the sure mercies of David.'**

Therefore He also says in another *Psalm:* **'You will not allow Your Holy One to see corruption.'**

"For David, after he had served his own generation by the will of God, fell asleep, was buried with his fathers, and saw corruption; but He whom God raised up saw no corruption. Therefore let it be known to you, brethren, that <u>**through this Man is preached to you the forgiveness of sins; and by Him everyone who believes is justified from all things from which you could not be justified by the law of Moses.**</u> Beware therefore, lest what has been spoken in the prophets come upon you: : **"<u>Behold, you despisers, marvel and perish</u>! For I work a work in your days, A work which you will by no means believe, though one were to declare it to you." Acts 13:16-41**

The religious leaders of Paul's time were strict followers of the law of Moses. They appeared holy and righteous, but they credited themselves as being <u>righteous by following the law, not the one who redeemed them from the curse of the law and fulfilled the righteous requirements of law, Jesus Christ</u>. Paul's missionary journeys were chosen by the Lord to reveal Christ to the people and through the Holy Spirit baptism, they would be able to have a personal relationship with Him and obey His leading of their lives. The Galatians were shown by Paul that to follow the law instead of the Spirit of God, brought them back to salvation through works and the "self" life. Paul preached about the death of the self life and declared the blessed life obtained through faith in Christ and the **obedience** of being **led by the Holy Spirit**.

"For as many as are led by the Spirit of God, these are the sons of God." **Rom. 8:14**

"O foolish Galatians! Who has **bewitched (cast a spell over you)** you that you **should not obey the truth,** before whose eyes Jesus Christ was clearly portrayed among you as crucified? This only I want to learn from you: Did you receive the Spirit by the works of the law, or by the hearing of faith? Are you so foolish? Having begun in the Spirit, are you now being made perfect by the flesh? Have you suffered so many things in vain—if indeed *it was* in vain?

Therefore He who supplies the Spirit to you and works miracles among you, *does He do it* by the works of the law, or by the hearing of faith?—just as Abraham "believed God, and it was accounted to him for righteousness." Therefore know that ***only* those who are of faith are sons of Abraham.** And the Scripture, foreseeing that God would **justify the Gentiles by faith,** preached the gospel to Abraham beforehand, *saying,* **"In you all the nations shall be blessed." So then those who *are* of faith are blessed with believing Abraham.**

For as many as are of **the works of the law are under the curse;**

for it is written, "**<u>Cursed *is* everyone who does not continue in all things which are written in the book of the law, to do them</u>**." But that **no one** is justified by the law in the sight of God *is* evident, for "**the just shall live by faith.**" Yet the law is not of faith, but **<u>"the man who does them shall live by them."</u>**

<u>Christ has redeemed us from the curse of the law,</u> <u>having become a curse for us</u> (for it is written, "Cursed *is* everyone who hangs on a tree"), that the <u>blessing of Abraham might come upon the Gentiles in Christ Jesus, that we might receive the promise of the Spirit through faith</u>. Brethren, I speak in the manner of men: Though *it is* only a man's covenant, yet *if it is* confirmed, no one annuls or adds to it. Now to Abraham and his Seed were the promises made. He does not say, "And to seeds," as of many, but as of one, "And to your Seed," who is Christ. And this I say, *that* the law, which was four hundred and thirty years later, cannot annul the covenant that was confirmed before by God in Christ, that it should make the promise of no effect. For if the inheritance *is* of the law, *it is* no longer of promise; but God gave *it* to Abraham by promise.

What purpose then *does* the law *serve?* It was added because of transgressions, till the Seed should come to whom the promise was made; *and it was* appointed through angels by the hand of a mediator. Now a mediator does not *mediate* for one *only,* but God is one.

Is the law then against the promises of God? Certainly not! For if there had been a law given which could have given life, truly righteousness would have been by the law. But the Scripture has confined all under sin, that the promise by faith in Jesus Christ might be given to those who believe. But before faith came, we were kept under guard by the law, kept for the faith which would afterward be revealed. Therefore the **law was our tutor *to bring us* to Christ, that we might be justified by faith. But after faith has come, we are no longer under a tutor.**

For you are all sons of God through faith in Christ Jesus. For as many of you as were baptized into Christ have put on Christ. There is neither Jew nor Greek, there is neither slave nor free, there is neither male nor female; **for you are all one in Christ Jesus. And if you *are* Christ's, then you are Abraham's seed, and heirs according to the promise." Gal. 3:1-29**

"The God of Abraham, Isaac, and Jacob, the God of our fathers, glorified His Servant Jesus, whom you delivered up and denied in the presence of Pilate, when he was determined to let *Him* go. But you denied the Holy One and the Just, and asked for a murderer to be granted to you, and killed the Prince of life, whom God raised from the dead, of which we are witnesses. And **His name, through faith in His name, has made this man strong, whom you see and know.** Yes, the faith which *comes* through Him has given him this perfect soundness in the presence of you all.

"Yet now, brethren, I know that you did *it* in ignorance, as *did* also your rulers. But those things which **God foretold** by the mouth of all His prophets, that the Christ would suffer, He has thus fulfilled. **Repent** therefore and be converted, that your sins may be blotted out, so that times of refreshing may come from the presence of the Lord, and that He may send Jesus Christ, who was preached to you before, whom heaven must receive until the times of restoration of all things, which God has spoken by the mouth of all His holy prophets since the world began. For Moses truly said to the fathers, **'The Lord your God will raise up for you a Prophet like me from your brethren. Him <u>you shall hear in all things, whatever He says to you</u>. And it shall be *that* every soul <u>who will not hear that Prophet</u> shall be utterly destroyed from among the people**.' Yes, and all the prophets, from Samuel and those who follow, as many as have spoken, have also foretold these days. You are sons of the prophets, and of the covenant which God made with our fathers, saying to Abraham, **'And in your seed** <u>all the families of the earth shall be blessed</u>.' To you first, God, having raised up His Servant Jesus, sent Him to **bless you**, in **turning away every one *of you* from your iniquities**." **Acts 3:1-26**

Jesus was sent to bless us in turning us away from our iniquities. He came to set the captives free and he whom the Son sets free is free indeed!

<u>JOSEPH</u>

"Now the birth of Jesus Christ was as follows: After His mother Mary was betrothed to Joseph, before they came together, she was found with child of the Holy Spirit. Then Joseph her husband, being a just man, and not wanting to make her a public example, was minded to put her away secretly. But while he thought about these things, behold an angel of the Lord appeared to him in a dream saying, "Joseph, son of David, do not be afraid to take to you Mary your wife, for that which is conceived in her is of the

Holy Spirit. And she will bring forth a Son, and you shall call His name Jesus, for He will save His people from their sins." So all this was done that it might be fulfilled **which was spoken by the Lord through the prophet**, saying: "Behold a virgin shall be with child, and will bear a Son, and they shall call His name Immanuel," which is translated, "God with us."

Then Joseph, being aroused from sleep, **did as the angel of the Lord commanded him** and took to him his wife, and did not know her till she had brought forth her firstborn Son. And he called His name Jesus." **Mat. 1:18-25**

This was an incredible test of trust that Joseph went through. The enemy was invading his thought life to put Mary away, but God released His truth, bringing freedom to him, when a divine visitation from the angel of the Lord, assured him regarding Jesus and released His directional plan to him. He actually saw the great honor of being chosen to be the earthly Father to the King of all Kings, Jesus Christ. He chose to obey the word of the Lord released to him.

MARY

Mary's response to the angel telling her she will have a son:

"Then Mary said, "Behold the maidservant of the Lord! Let it be to me according to your word."

Mary obeyed the word of the Lord and delivered the Messiah, Jesus, the Savior of the world!

CHAPTER 6

PERFECT OBEDIENCE

JESUS CHRIST (KING OF KINGS)

There is a powerful word of truth that was released through Mary, the mother of Jesus during the wedding of Cana when Jesus began his miracle ministry.

"On the third day there was a wedding in Cana of Galilee, and the mother of Jesus was there. Now both Jesus and His disciples were invited to the wedding. And when they ran out of wine, the mother of Jesus said to Him, "They have no wine."

Jesus said to her, "Woman, what does your concern have to do with Me? My hour has not yet come." His mother said to the servants, **"Whatever He says to you, do it."**

Now there were set there six waterpots of stone, according to the manner of purification of the Jews, containing twenty or thirty gallons apiece. Jesus said to them, "Fill the waterpots with water." And they filled them up to the brim. And He said to them, **"Draw *some* out now, and take *it* to the master of the feast."** And they took *it.* When the master of the feast had tasted the water that was made wine, and did not know where it came from (but the servants who had drawn the water knew), the master of the feast called the bridegroom. And he said to him, "Every man at the beginning sets out the good wine, and when the *guests* have well drunk, then the inferior. You have kept the **good wine** until now!"

This beginning of signs Jesus did in Cana of Galilee, and manifested His glory; and His disciples believed in Him. After this

He went down to Capernaum, He, His mother, His brothers, and His disciples; and they did not stay there many days."
John 2:1-12

Obedience to His word brought a supernatural miracle.

But Diane, that was His mother, he did miracles for her to honor her. Look at this truth:

"For whoever does the will of My Father in heaven is My brother and sister and mother." Mat. 12:50

"Enter by the **narrow gate;** for **wide *is* the gate and broad *is* the way that leads to destruction**, and there are **many** who go in by it. Because **narrow *is* the gate and difficult *is* the way which leads to life, and there are few who find it.**

"Beware of false prophets, who come to you in sheep's clothing, but **inwardly** they are ravenous wolves. You will know them by their fruits. Do men gather grapes from thorn bushes or figs from thistles? Even so, every good tree bears good fruit, but a bad tree bears bad fruit. A good tree **cannot** bear bad fruit, nor can a bad tree bear good fruit. **Every tree that does not bear good fruit is cut down and thrown into the fire.** Therefore **by their fruits** you will **know them**.

I NEVER KNEW YOU

"**Not everyone** who says to Me, 'Lord, Lord,' shall enter the kingdom of heaven, but **he who does the will of My Father in heaven**. **Many will say to Me in that day**, 'Lord, Lord, have we not prophesied in Your name, cast out demons in Your name, and done many wonders in Your name?' And then I will declare to them, '**<u>I never knew you; depart from Me</u>, you who <u>practice lawlessness</u>**!' **Mat. 7:13-23**

"<u>Whoever commits sin also commits lawlessness, and sin is lawlessness</u>. And you know that He was manifested to take away our sins, and in Him there is no sin. Whoever abides in Him does not sin. Whoever sins has neither seen Him nor known Him. Little children, let no one deceive you. He who <u>practices righteousness is righteous, just as He is righteous</u>. **He who sins is of the devil, for the devil has sinned from the beginning. <u>For this purpose</u>** the Son of God was manifested, that He might <u>destroy the works of the devil</u>." **1 Jn. 3:4-8**

"Therefore whoever **<u>hears these sayings of Mine, and does them</u>**, I will liken him to a **<u>wise man</u>** who built his house on the **rock**: and the rain descended, the floods came, and the winds blew and beat on that house; and it **did not fall**, for it was **founded on the rock**.

"But everyone who hears these sayings of Mine, and **<u>does not do them</u>**, will be like a **<u>foolish man</u>** who built his house on the **sand**: and the rain descended, the floods came, and the winds blew and beat on that house; and it fell. And **<u>great was its fall</u>**." And so it was, when Jesus had ended these sayings, that the people were astonished at His teaching, for He taught them as one having authority, and not as the scribes." **Mat. 7:24-29**

<u>WHAT IS THE FATHER'S WILL?</u>

"Then it shall come to pass, because you **<u>listen to these</u>**

judgments, and keep and do them, that the Lord your God will **keep with you the covenant and the mercy which He swore to your fathers**. And He will **love you and bless you and multiply you**; He will also **bless the fruit of your womb** and the **fruit of your land**, your **grain and your new wine and your oil**, the increase of your **cattle and the offspring of your flock**, in the land of which He swore to your fathers to give you. You shall be **blessed above all peoples**; there shall not be a **male or female barren among you or among your livestock**. And **the Lord will take away from you all sickness, and will afflict you with none of the terrible diseases of Egypt which you have known, but will lay them on all those who hate you." Deut. 7:12-15**

Listening, keeping and doing of the law of the Lord caused His blessings to come to the Israelites in every area of their lives and the Lord honored His covenant keeping promise to them when He rescued them from Egypt. In Christ we are adopted into the faith as sons and daughters. Christ came to **fulfill the law** through His obedience to everything His Father told Him to do. **Obedience to His commands** will bring increase to our lives. **The opposite truth applies to disobedience.**

"If a man has a stubborn and rebellious son who will not obey the voice of his father or the voice of his mother, and who, when they have chastened him, will not heed them, then his father and his mother shall take hold of him and bring him out to the elders of his city, to the gate of his city. And they shall say to the elders of his city, 'This son of ours is stubborn and rebellious; he will not obey our voice; he is a

glutton and a drunkard.' Then all the men of his city shall stone him to death with stones; so you shall put away the evil from among you, and all Israel shall hear and fear." Deut. 21:18-21 The law required **<u>death for rebellion</u>.**

Thank You Father, for sending your Son Jesus, who died on the cross to pay our price tag for rebellion and disobedience!

Now you will see a scripture that's been used for years, many times regarding finances, that has so much more meaning to us.

"Yet from the days of your fathers You have gone away from My ordinances and <u>have not kept them</u>. Return to Me, and I will return to you," Says the Lord of hosts. "But you said, 'In what way shall we return?' "Will a man rob God? Yet you have robbed Me! But you say, 'In what way have we robbed You?' **In tithes and offerings.** You are cursed with a curse, for you have robbed Me, Even this whole nation. Bring all the tithes into the storehouse, that there may be food in My house,
And try Me now in this," says the Lord of hosts, "If I will not open for you the windows of heaven
And pour out for you ***such*** **blessing** that *there* **<u>will not be room enough to receive it</u>.**

"And <u>I will rebuke the devourer for your sakes</u>, <u>So that he will not destroy the fruit of your ground,</u>
<u>Nor shall the vine fail to bear fruit for you in the field</u>," Says the Lord of hosts; "And **all nations will call you <u>blessed</u>**, For you will be a delightful land," Says the Lord of hosts." **Mal. 3:7-10**

"Do not be deceived, God is not mocked; for **<u>whatever a man</u>**

sows, that he will also reap." **Gal. 6:7**

"All things have been delivered to Me by My Father, and no one knows the Son except the Father. Nor does anyone know the Father except the Son, and *the one* to whom the Son wills to reveal Him." Lk. 10:22

"When Jesus came into the region of Caesarea Philippi, He asked His disciples, saying, "Who do men say that I, the Son of Man, am?" So they said, "Some say John the Baptist, some Elijah, and others Jeremiah or one of the prophets." He said to them, "But who do you say that I am?" Simon Peter answered and said, "**You are the Christ, the Son of the living God**." Jesus answered and said to him, "Blessed are you, Simon Bar-Jonah, for flesh and blood has not revealed this to you, but **My Father who is in heaven**. And I also say to you that you are Peter, and on this rock I will build My church, and the **gates of Hades shall not prevail against it.** And I will give you the keys of the kingdom of heaven, and whatever you bind on earth will be bound in heaven, and whatever you loose on earth will be loosed in heaven."

Jesus explains to Peter the divine revelation granted to those who know Him and do the **will of the Father.**

"At that time the disciples came to Jesus, saying, "Who then is greatest in the kingdom of heaven?"

Then Jesus called **a little child to Him**, set him in the midst of them, and said, "Assuredly, I say to you, unless you are **converted and become as little children**, you will by no means enter the kingdom of heaven. Therefore whoever **humbles himself as this**

little child <u>is the greatest</u> in the kingdom of heaven. **Whoever receives one little child like this in My name <u>receives Me</u>**.

<u>FORGIVE YOUR OFFENDER</u>

"But whoever causes one of these little ones who believe in Me to sin, it would be better for him if a millstone were hung around his neck, and he were drowned in the depth of the sea. Woe to the world because of offenses! For offenses must come, but <u>woe to that man by whom the offense comes</u>! "If your hand or foot causes you to sin, cut it off and cast it from you. It is better for you to enter into life lame or maimed, rather than having two hands or two feet, to be cast into the everlasting fire. And if your eye causes you to sin, pluck it out and cast it from you. It is better for you to enter into life with one eye, rather than having two eyes, to be cast into hell fire."

<u>WIN AND LOVE THE LOST</u>

"Take heed that you do not despise one of these little ones, for I say to you that in heaven their angels always see the face of My Father who is in heaven. For the Son of Man has come to save that which was lost. "What do you think? If a man has a hundred sheep, and one of them goes astray, does he not leave the ninety-nine and go to the mountains to seek the one that is straying? And if he should find it, assuredly, I say to you, he rejoices more over that sheep than over the ninety-nine that did not go astray. Even so it is **<u>not the will of your Father who is in heaven that one of these little ones should perish</u>.**

FORGIVE THE SINNER

"Moreover if your brother sins against you, go and tell him his fault between you and him alone. If he hears you, you have gained your brother. But if he will not hear, take with you one or two more, that 'by the mouth of two or three witnesses every word may be established.' And if he refuses to hear them, tell *it* to the church. But if he refuses even to hear the church, let him be to you like a heathen and a tax collector.

"**Assuredly, I say to you, whatever you bind on earth will be bound in heaven, and whatever you loose on earth will be loosed in heaven. "Again I say to you that if two of you agree on earth concerning anything that they ask, it will be done for them by My Father in heaven. For where two or three are gathered together in My name, I am there in the midst of them**." **Mat. 18:1-20**

Where there is agreement in Lord's **will and purpose**, it produces the agreement in the Lord's **manifested presence and power**. Forgiveness is a choice to obey the word of God. It has nothing to do with feelings. I cover this subject fully in my book: "**Jesus Breaks the Chain of Offense**" where I received a divine revelation regarding offenses. The message the Lord released to me changed me forever and you **can** be offense free!!!!

JESUS OBEYS HIS FATHER'S WILL

Then Jesus came with them to a place called Gethsemane, and said to the disciples, "Sit here while I go and pray over there." And He took with Him Peter and the two sons of Zebedee, and He began to be sorrowful and deeply distressed. Then He said to them, "My soul is exceedingly sorrowful, even to death. Stay here and watch with Me."

He went a little farther and fell on His face, and prayed, saying, "O My Father, if it is possible, let this cup pass from Me; nevertheless, **not as I will, but as You will**."

Then He came to the disciples and found them sleeping, and said to Peter, "What! Could you not watch with Me one hour? **Watch and pray, lest you enter into temptation. The spirit indeed *is* willing, but the flesh is weak."**

Again, a second time, He went away and prayed, saying, "O My Father, if this cup cannot pass away from Me unless I drink it, **Your will be done.**" **Mat. 26:36-42**

The greatest obedience of all time came with the man Jesus. This man was willing to lay aside His deity and willingly came to this earth for you and me for the divine purpose of the Father's command to be fulfilled. He knew that without the shedding of blood from a spotless lamb for sin's sacrifice, there would be no remission for sin. What an incredible price was paid by our Lord for us. Why would He pay such a horrific price for us?

"For God so loved the world that He gave His only begotten Son, that whoever believes in Him should not perish but have everlasting life. For God did not send His Son into the world to condemn the world, but that the world through Him might be saved. He who believes in Him is not condemned; but he who does not believe is condemned already, because he has not believed in the name of the only begotten Son of God. And this is the condemnation, that the light has come into the world , and

men loved darkness rather than light, because their deeds were evil. For everyone **practicing evil** hates the light and does not come to the light, lest his deeds should be exposed. But he who does the truth comes to the light, that his deeds may be clearly seen, that they have been done in God." **Jn. 3:16-21**

"For whoever is ashamed of Me and **My words** in this adulterous and sinful generation, of him the Son of Man also will be ashamed when He comes in the glory of His Father with the holy angels." **Mk. 8:38**

KEEP HIS WORD

This Book of the Law **shall not depart from your mouth**, but you shall meditate in it day and night, that you may observe to do according to all that is written in it. For then you will make your way prosperous, and then you will have good success. **Have I not commanded you?** Be strong and of good courage; do not be afraid, nor be dismayed, for the Lord your God *is* with you wherever you go." **Josh. 1:8-9**

"He who does not love Me does not **keep My words**; and the word which you hear is not Mine but **the Father's** who sent Me." **Jn. 14:24**

"One who **turns away his ear from hearing the law**, even his prayer *is* an abomination." **Prov. 28:9**

And He **said to those who sold doves, "Take these things away! Do not make My Father's house a house of merchandise!" Jn. 2:16**

"I can of My**self do nothing. As I hear, I judge; and** My

judgment is righteous, because I do not seek My own will but the will of the Father who sent Me." Jn.5:30

"Finally then, brethren, we urge and exhort in the Lord Jesus that you should abound more and more, just as you received from us **how you ought to walk and to please God**; for you know what commandments we gave you through the Lord Jesus.

"For **this is the will of God, your sanctification:** that you should abstain from sexual immorality; that each of you should know how to possess his own vessel in sanctification and honor, not in passion of lust, like the Gentiles who do not know God; that no one should take advantage of and defraud his brother in this matter, because the Lord *is* the avenger of all such, as we also forewarned you and testified. For God did not call us to uncleanness, but in holiness. Therefore he who **rejects *this* does not reject man, but God, who has also given us His Holy Spirit." 1Thes. 4:3-7**

"Grace to you and peace from God the Father and our Lord Jesus Christ, who gave Himself for our sins, that He might deliver us from this present evil age, **according to the will of our God and Father, to whom *be* glory forever and ever. Amen." Gal. 1:1-4**

"Dare any of you, having a matter against another, go to law before the unrighteous, and not before the saints? Do you not know that the saints will judge the world? And if the world will be judged by you, are you unworthy to judge the smallest matters? Do you not know that we shall judge angels? How much more, things that pertain to this life? If then you have judgments concerning things pertaining to this life, do you appoint those who are least esteemed by the church to judge? I say this to your shame. Is it so, that there is not a wise man among you, not even one, who will be able to judge between his brethren? But **brother goes to law against brother, and that before unbelievers!**

Now therefore, it is already an utter failure for you that you go to law against one another. Why do you not rather accept wrong? Why do you not rather *let yourselves* be cheated? No, you yourselves do wrong and cheat, and *you do* these things *to your* brethren! Do you not know that the unrighteous will not inherit the kingdom of God? Do not be deceived. Neither fornicators, nor idolaters, nor adulterers, nor homosexuals, nor sodomites, nor thieves, nor covetous, nor drunkards, nor revilers, nor extortioners will inherit the kingdom of God. And such **were** some of you. But you were washed, but you were **sanctified**, but you were **justified in the name of the Lord Jesus and by the Spirit of our God**." **1 Cor. 6:1-11**

"In everything give thanks; for this is the will of God in Christ Jesus for you." 1 Thes. 5:18

"I beseech you therefore brethren, by the mercies of God, that you present your bodies a living sacrifice, holy, acceptable to God, which is your reasonable service. And **do not be conformed to this world, but be transformed by the renewing of your mind**, that you may prove what is that **good and acceptable and perfect will of God**." **Rom. 12:1-2**

CHAPTER 7

THE LORD'S RETURN

"Then the kingdom of heaven shall be likened to ten virgins who took their lamps and went out to meet the bridegroom. Now five of them were **wise**, and five were **foolish.** Those who were foolish took their lamps and took no oil with them, but the wise took oil in their vessels with their lamps. But while the bridegroom was delayed, they all **slumbered and slept**.

"And at midnight a cry was heard: **'Behold, the bridegroom is coming; go out to meet him!'** Then all those virgins arose and trimmed their lamps. And the foolish said to the wise, 'Give us some of your oil, for our lamps are going out.' But the wise answered, saying, '**No, lest there should not be enough for us and you; but go rather to those who sell, and buy for yourselves**.' And while they went to buy, **the bridegroom came**, and those who were ready went in with him to the wedding; and the **door was shut**. Afterward the other virgins came also, saying, 'Lord, Lord, open to us!' But he answered and said, 'Assuredly, I say to you, **I do not know you**.' "Watch therefore, for you know neither the day nor the hour in which the Son of Man is coming." **Mat. 25:1-13**

"But **I do not want you to be ignorant**, brethren, concerning those who have fallen asleep, lest you sorrow as others who have no hope. For **if we believe that Jesus died and rose again, even so God will bring with Him those who sleep in Jesus.**

For this we say to you by the word of the Lord, that we who are alive *and* remain until the coming of the Lord will by no means precede those who are asleep. For the Lord Himself will descend from heaven with a shout, with the voice of an archangel, and with the trumpet of God. And the dead in Christ will rise first. Then we who are alive *and* remain shall be caught up together with them in the clouds to meet the Lord in the air. And thus we shall always be with the Lord. Therefore comfort one another with these words." **1 Thess. 4:13-18**

VISION GIVEN TO ME IN INTERCESSION LAST YEAR:

Vision given to Diane Bernardin March 3, 2018:

"I saw a massive flow of fire coming from heaven toward the earth with rippling waves that moved as if they were living. As it came toward the tent that is going up in April. I knew in my spirit that the Lord sent the fire and He spoke to my heart: that this fire will consume all that defiles.

As I have shared it with others, the Lord added that it will cleanse and purge His people. **Malachi 3:1-**

Apostle Willie Walker shared:

New Living Translation

“When Solomon finished praying, fire flashed down from heaven and burned up the burnt offerings and sacrifices, and the glorious presence of the LORD filled the Temple. **2 Chronicles 7:1** ” Come Holy Spirit!!!

On February 15th, 2019 this word was given to me, so I include it with this vision He showed me last year:

"For I am about to bring my people into a place of a fiery furnace where I will burn out the chaff. I will burn out the bondage they have been holding onto for years. And when they are refined, I will pull them out and rescue them and I will pour my oil upon them and use them to set the captives free."

“And you shall take the anointing oil, pour it on his head, and anoint him. **Exodus 29:7**

DOES HE KNOW YOU?

This is the **most important question** that is asked throughout scripture to each one of us. You may answer, “I've been saved since I was a child and listened to many thousands of sermons preached and I am a loyal member of so and so church and I attend my church every Sunday. I was raised in the church!” This question is not about a prayer you said as a child or an adult. It has nothing to do with attending a church. Think about what your answer would be to that question because that most important answer will determine your “**true salvation” vs. your “escape**

from hell" salvation. After reading these scriptures for yourself, it should be **so clear** what the Lord would say to you. I pray your eyes have been opened to His **very sobering truth**.

I **will not** add one thing to these words, as they speak from the heart the Father, and with fear and trembling I release them to you. These are the words He wanted each one of you to learn and share with others. I am sure there will be many that you know are not ready for His return. Do you care enough about them to tell them or share this book of truth with them? The book only reveals the truth written in His word. I have only sectioned the subject matter so you can see that throughout the entire Bible this subject is discussed. The truth is there and the choice **only you will make**. You will stand **alone** before Him one day, just as I will.

Now I present you that most important question of all: **"Do you know Him?"** You see I cannot answer for you as the choice is totally yours; whether to surrender to Him and be confident that you do know Him and are prepared to meet Him at His arrival. Whether you meet Him through your appointed date of death or the rapture of the church; it really won't matter which will come first, if you are truly ready to meet Him when He says it's your time. Please search your heart as I have searched mine.

Should you not see yourself as ready, I have wonderful news for you. There is a way to know that you know, you are ready to meet Him. True repentance is the answer. A casual I'm sorry Lord is **not** true repentance. The word means: **sincere regret or remorse, contrition, contriteness, penitence, sorrow,**

sorrowfulness, regret, ruefulness, remorsefulness, pangs of conscience, prickings of conscience, shame, guilt, self-reproach, self-condemnation and conversion.

There is **no chain of bondage He cannot break,** there is **no sin he cannot forgive**, there is **no sickness or heartache that He cannot heal**, if you surrender it all over to Him. He never designed you or I to carry that **guilt and shame**, His desire is healing, love, joy, peace, longsuffering, kindness, goodness, faithfulness, gentleness and self-control as our fruit. **Gal. 5:22,23**

Are you living with His fruit ripe on your tree of life, ready for anyone, especially the lost to pick from?

"For this is the covenant that I will make with the house of Israel after those days, says the Lord: I will put My laws in their mind and <u>write them on their hearts</u>; and I will be their God, and they shall be My people." **Heb. 8:10**

HEALING TESTIMONY FROM OBEYING THE LORD

I want to share a great testimony that happened recently which resulted from a choice to obey the Lord's voice. My husband Michel was invited to come to a local church to minister the word and ended in prayer for the people. There was a lady there named Debbie Spear who Michel prayed for and she told me as she was leaving that she felt the presence of God touch her leg twice after Michel prayed for her, but the full healing hadn't yet manifested. I asked her what was going on with her leg that the presence of God touched her and she told me the doctor believed she had scoliosis (which is an abnormal curvature of the spine) and she couldn't sit up in a chair, she would lean over to one side. One of her legs had been 4-6 inches longer than the other so she walked with an incredible limp. As she was sharing with me. the Holy Spirit spoke to my spirit and said: "Sit her down in a chair up front and pray for her legs."

Well I had never done that before, I had only seen it done in a Charles and Francis Hunter service years ago. When she stretched out her legs as far as she could, the vast difference in length was seen. I closed my eyes and prayed: Lord Jesus you are the healer and we agree for Your healing power to grow out her leg that is shorter so the legs could be even and balanced in Jesus' name, amen." I opened my eyes and asked her 2 friends with us if there was any change and she said, not really but something is starting to happen. Keep praying. So I closed my eyes again and said, "Lord Jesus, be glorified in this healing for Your daughter. Thank you for making everything in normal balance for Your name sake amen." Well I opened my eyes and to my amazement, the legs were absolutely normal in length and the Lord restored her. What I didn't know is that the problem went up the entire right side of her body and she was instantly healed!"

Here's Debbie's testimony: **(Taken from Facebook)**

Who remembers this photo post?

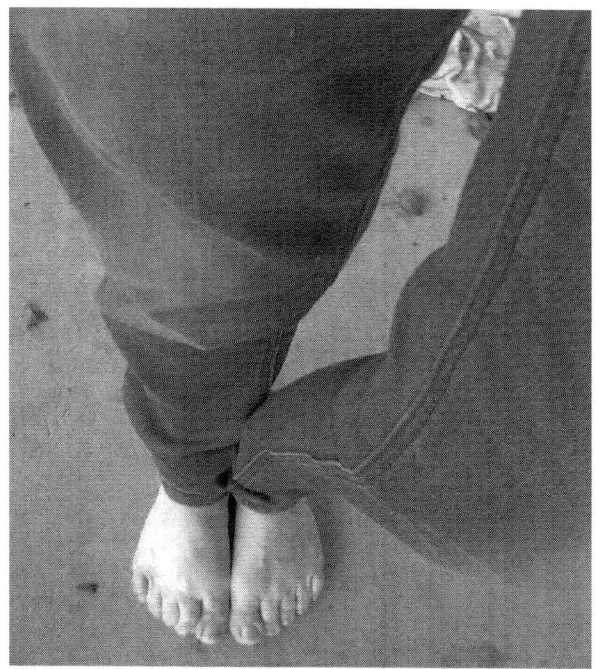

Well, I have a ~PRAISE~ Report!

Bishop Michael and Diane Bernardin of CrossSounds Ministries were there this evening, and I thank God for it. He was laying on of hands tonight on our legs from the feet up to our knees. When he got to me, I felt the power of our Lord from my toes to the bottom of my knee. Twice he did that, twice I felt that.

A little bit later I was talking to Diane about my short leg. So she had me sit down. She put her hands on my on my feet when I saw my right LEG IS NOW THE SAME LENGTH AS MY LEFT LEG!! Guess what else... My right arm is now the SAME LENGTH AS MY LEFT ARM!!

HALLELUJAH, thank you LORD!

Now I almost have to learn how to walk again with legs the same length!

Debbie Spear 5/26/2019

TWO YEARS EARLIER:

September 13, 2017

"Well, here goes.... Whatever it is, it continues to get worse. I've talked to Dr. Chandler many, many times about the shrinking of my right side. (Right side hair follicles, arm, hand and fingers, breast, leg, foot/toes.) I never get answers. Last time I was there she says **scoliosis**. Well of course might be now, with my spine is getting more and more crooked since my legs aren't the same length and hips not parallel. Yesterday, after all this time, some pain is starting in right hip. I would really like some answers. I would like to know if there is a way to stop it., etcetera. My hips is straight in picture. **BEFORE PICTURE ABOVE**

My leg is still a lot thinner than the other still, along with the rest of my right side, including my hip. If I sit evenly I lean a lot towards the right.

THIS IS AN UNDENIABLE MIRACLE FROM OUR LORD

TO GOD BE THE GLORY AND ALL THE PRAISE FOR THE GREAT MIRACLE **HE DID FOR DEBBIE**.

"How God anointed Jesus of Nazareth with the Holy Spirit and with power, who went about doing good and healing all who were oppressed by the devil, for God was with Him." **Acts 10:38**

"Most assuredly, I say to you he who believes in Me, the works that I do he will do also; and greater works than these he will do because I go to My Father." **Jn. 14:12**

CHAPTER 8

THE LORD'S HEART TOWARD YOU

"**Woe to the rebellious children**," says the Lord, "**Who take counsel, but not of Me,**
And who **devise plans, but not of My Spirit, That they may add sin to sin**;
Who walk to go down to Egypt, And **have not asked My advice**,
To strengthen themselves in the strength of Pharaoh, And to trust in the shadow of Egypt!
Therefore the strength of Pharaoh shall be your shame, and trust in the shadow of Egypt shall be your humiliation. For his princes were at Zoan, and his ambassadors came to Hanes.
They were all ashamed of a people who could not benefit them,
Or be help or benefit, but a shame and also a reproach."

The burden against the beasts of the South. Through a land of trouble and anguish, from which came the lioness and lion, the viper and fiery flying serpent, they will carry their riches on the backs of young donkeys, And their treasures on the humps of camels, to a people who shall not profit; for the Egyptians shall help in vain and to no purpose. Therefore I have called her Rahab-Hem-Shebeth. Now go, **write it before them on a tablet, And note it on a scroll, that it may be for time to come, forever and ever: That this is a rebellious people, lying children, children who will not hear the law of the Lord;** Who say to the seers, "**Do not see**," And to the prophets, "**Do not prophesy to us right things; Speak to us smooth things, prophesy deceits. Get out of the way, Turn aside from the**

path, Cause the Holy One of Israel to cease from before us."

Therefore thus says the Holy One of Israel: "Because you despise this word, and **trust in oppression and perversity, and rely on them, Therefore this iniquity shall be to you like a breach ready to fall, a bulge in a high wall, whose breaking comes suddenly, in an instant.**
And He shall break it like the breaking of the potter's vessel, which is broken in pieces;
He shall not spare. So there shall not be found among its fragments, a shard to take fire from the hearth, or to take water from the cistern."

For thus says the Lord God, the Holy One of Israel: "**In returning and rest you shall be saved; In quietness and confidence shall be your strength**."
But you would not, and you said, "No, for we will flee on horses"—Therefore you shall flee!
And, "We will ride on swift *horses*"—Therefore those who pursue you shall be swift! One thousand *shall flee* at the threat of one, at the threat of five you shall flee, till you are left as a pole on top of a mountain and as a banner on a hill.

Therefore **the Lord will wait, that He may be gracious to you; and therefore He will be exalted, that He may have mercy on you. For the Lord *is* a God of justice; Blessed *are* all those who wait for Him.**
For the people shall dwell in Zion at Jerusalem; you shall weep no more.
He will be very gracious to you at the sound of your cry;

When He hears it, He will answer you. And *though* **the Lord gives you the bread of adversity and the water of affliction,** Yet your teachers will not be moved into a corner anymore, but **your eyes shall see your teachers. Your ears shall hear a word behind you, saying, "This *is* the way, walk in it,"** whenever you turn to the right hand or whenever you turn to the left. You will also defile the covering of your images of silver, and the ornament of your molded images of gold.
You will throw them away as an unclean thing; you will say to them, "Get away!"
Then He will give the rain for your seed with which you sow the ground, and bread of the increase of the earth; It will be fat and plentiful. In that day your cattle will feed in large pastures.
Likewise the oxen and the young donkeys that work the ground will eat cured fodder,
which has been winnowed with the shovel and fan. There will be on every high mountain and on every high hill rivers *and* streams of waters, In the day of the great slaughter, **when the towers fall.** Moreover the light of the moon will be as the light of the sun, and the light of the sun will be sevenfold, as the light of seven days, in the day that the Lord binds up the bruise of His people
and heals the stroke of their wound. **"Wash yourselves, make yourselves clean; Put away the evil of your doings from before My eyes. Cease to do evil, learn to do good; seek justice, rebuke the oppressor; defend the fatherless, plead for the widow.**
"Come now, and let us reason together," says the Lord,
"**Though your sins are like scarlet,**
They shall be as white as snow; Though they are red like

crimson, they shall be as wool.
If you are willing and obedient, you shall eat the good of the land; But if you refuse and rebel, you shall be devoured by the sword"; For the mouth of the Lord has spoken." Isa. 1:16-20
"For the wages of sin is death, but the gift of God is **eternal life in Christ Jesus our Lord." Rom. 6:23**
Without Jesus Christ laying down His own life for our sin, we had no hope. Our own good works could not earn us eternal life. In the old covenant stood the tabernacle of Moses, where the high priest was the only person able to bring the atonement for sin by shedding of the blood of animals. In the New Covenant, **Jesus Christ became the sinless lamb, shedding His blood for us as a living sacrifice, all because of love.**

"Then indeed, even the first *covenant* had ordinances of divine service and the earthly sanctuary. For a tabernacle was prepared: the first *part,* in which *was* the lampstand, the table, and the showbread, which is called the sanctuary; and behind the second veil, the part of the tabernacle which is called the Holiest of All, which had the golden censer and the ark of the covenant overlaid on all sides with gold, in which *were* the golden pot that had the manna, Aaron's rod that budded, and the tablets of the covenant; and above it were the cherubim of glory overshadowing the mercy seat. Of these things we cannot now speak in detail.
Now when these things had been thus prepared, the priests always went into the first part of the tabernacle, performing the services. But into the **second part the high priest *went* alone once a year, not without blood, which he offered for himself**

and *for* the people's sins *committed* in ignorance; the Holy Spirit indicating this, that the way into the Holiest of All was not yet made manifest while the first tabernacle was still standing. It *was* symbolic for the present time in which both gifts and sacrifices are offered which cannot make him who performed the service perfect in regard to the conscience—*concerned* only with foods and drinks, various washings, and fleshly ordinances imposed until the time of reformation.

But **Christ came *as* High Priest** of the good things to come, with the greater and more perfect tabernacle not made with hands, that is, not of this creation. Not with the blood of goats and calves, but with **His own blood** He entered the Most Holy Place **once for all**, having obtained eternal redemption. For if the blood of bulls and goats and the ashes of a heifer, sprinkling the unclean, sanctifies for the purifying of the flesh, **how much more shall the blood of Christ, who through the eternal Spirit offered Himself without spot to God, cleanse your conscience from dead works to serve the living God?** And for this reason **He is the Mediator** of the new covenant, by means of death, for the redemption of the transgressions under the first covenant, that those who are called may receive the promise of the eternal inheritance. For where there is a testament, there must also of necessity be the death of the testator. For a testament is in force after men are dead, since it has no power at all while the testator lives. Therefore not even the first covenant was dedicated without blood. For when Moses had spoken every precept to all the people according to the law, he took the blood of calves and goats, with water, scarlet wool, and hyssop, and sprinkled both the book itself and all the people, saying, "This is the blood of the covenant which God has commanded you." Then likewise he sprinkled with blood both the tabernacle and all the vessels of the ministry. And according to the law almost all things are purified with blood, and **without shedding of blood there is no remission.**

Therefore it was necessary that the copies of the things in the heavens should be purified with these, but the heavenly things themselves with better sacrifices than these. For Christ has not entered the holy places made with hands, which are copies of the true, but into heaven itself, now to appear in the presence of God for us; not that He should offer Himself often, as the high priest enters the Most Holy Place every year with blood of another—He then would have had to suffer often since the foundation of the world; but now, once at the end of the ages, **He has appeared to put away sin by the sacrifice of Himself**. And as **it is appointed for men to die once, but after this the judgment, so Christ was offered once to bear the sins of many. To those who eagerly wait for Him He will appear a second time, apart from sin, for salvation**." **Heb. 9:1-28**

"For by grace you have been saved through faith, and that not of yourselves; *it is* the **gift of God, not of works, lest anyone should boast**. For we are His workmanship, created in Christ Jesus **for good works, which God prepared beforehand that we should walk in them." Eph. 2:9-10**

Jesus said, "Come to Me, all *you* who labor and are heavy laden, and I will give you rest. **Take My yoke upon you and learn from**

Me, for I am gentle and lowly in heart, and you will find rest for your souls. For My yoke *is* easy and My burden is light." Mat. 11:28-30

ETERNAL LIFE WITH CHRIST

Whoever believes that Jesus is the Christ is born of God, and **everyone who loves Him who begot also loves him who is begotten of Him**. By this we know that we love the children of God, when we **love God and keep His commandments**. For **this is the love of God**, that we keep His commandments. And His commandments are not burdensome. For whatever is born of God overcomes the world. And this is the victory that has overcome the world—**our faith**. Who is he who overcomes the world, but **he who believes that Jesus is the Son of God**?

This is He who came by **water and blood—Jesus Christ; not only by water, but by water and blood**. And it is the Spirit who bears witness, because the Spirit is truth. For there are three that bear witness in heaven: **the Father, the Word, and the Holy Spirit**; and **these three are one**. And there are **three** that bear witness on earth: **the Spirit, the water, and the blood; and these three agree as one**. If we receive the witness of men, the witness of God is greater; for this is the witness of God which He has testified of His Son. He who believes in the Son of God has the witness in himself; he who does not believe God **has made Him a liar**, because he has not believed the testimony that God has given of His Son. And this is the testimony: **that God has given us eternal life, and this life is in His Son**. He who has the Son **has life**; he who does not have the Son of God **does not have life**.

These things I have written to **you who believe in the name of the Son of God**, that you may **know that you have eternal life**, and that you may ***continue to*** **believe in the name of the Son of God.**

Now this is the confidence that we have in Him, that **if we ask anything according to His will, He hears us. And if we know that He hears us, whatever we ask, we know that we have the petitions that we have asked of Him.** If anyone sees his brother sinning a sin *which does* not *lead* to death, he will ask, and He will give him life for those who commit sin not *leading* to death. There is sin *leading* to death. I do not say that he should pray about that. **All unrighteousness is sin**, and there is sin not *leading* to death.

We know that whoever is **born of God does not sin**; but **he who has been born of God keeps himself, and the wicked one does not touch him**. We know that we are of God, and the whole world lies *under the sway of* the wicked one. And we know that the **Son of God has come and has given us an understanding, that we may know Him who is true; and we are in Him who is true, in His Son Jesus Christ. This is the true God and eternal life. Little children, keep yourselves from idols. Amen**." **1 Jn 5:1-21**

"Blessed *is* the man who **endures temptation**; for when he has been approved, he will receive the **crown of life** which the Lord has promised to those **who love Him**. Let no one say when he is tempted, "I am tempted by God"; for God cannot be tempted by evil, nor does He Himself tempt anyone. But each one is tempted **when he is drawn away by his own desires and enticed**. Then, when desire has conceived, it gives birth to sin; and sin, when it is full-grown, brings forth death.

Do not be deceived, my beloved brethren. Every good gift and every perfect gift is from above, and comes down from the **Father of lights**, with whom there is no variation or shadow of turning. Of His own will **He brought us forth by the word of truth,** that **we might be a kind of first fruits of His creatures**. So then, my beloved brethren, let every man be **swift to hear, slow to speak, slow to wrath; for the wrath of man does not produce the righteousness of God**.

Therefore **lay aside all filthiness and overflow of wickedness, and receive with meekness the implanted word, which is able to save your souls**. But be **doers of the word, and not hearers only**, **deceiving yourselves**. For if anyone is a hearer of the word and **not a doer**, he is like a man observing his natural face in a mirror; for he observes himself, goes away, and immediately forgets what kind of man he was. But he who looks into the perfect law of liberty and continues in it, and is not a forgetful hearer but a **doer of the work, this one will be blessed in what he does**.

If anyone among you **thinks he is religious**, and **does not bridle his tongue but deceives his own heart, this one's religion *is* useless**. Pure and undefiled religion before God and the Father is this: **to visit orphans and widows in their trouble, *and* to keep oneself unspotted from the world**. **Jas.1:12-27**

RECEIVE CHRIST AS YOUR SAVIOR

"Brethren, my heart's desire and prayer to God for Israel is that **they may be saved**. For I bear them witness that they have a zeal for God, but not according to knowledge. For they being ignorant of God's righteousness, and seeking to establish their own righteousness, have not submitted to the righteousness of God. For Christ is the end of the law for righteousness to everyone who believes.

For Moses writes about the righteousness which is of the law, "The man who does those things shall live by them." But the righteousness of faith speaks in this way, "Do not say in your heart, 'Who will ascend into heaven?' " (that is, to bring Christ down from above) or, "'Who will descend into the abyss?' " (that is, to bring Christ up from the dead). But what does it say? "The word is near you, in your mouth and in your heart" (that is, the word of faith which we preach): that if you **confess with your mouth the Lord Jesus and believe in your heart that God has raised Him from the dead, you will be saved**. **For with the heart one believes unto righteousness, and with the mouth confession is made unto salvation**. For the Scripture says, "**Whoever believes on Him will not be put to shame." For there is no distinction between Jew and Greek, for the same Lord over all is rich to all who call upon Him. For "whoever calls on the name of the Lord shall be saved**."

How then shall they call on Him in whom they have not believed? And how shall they believe in Him of whom they have not heard? And how shall they hear without a preacher? And how shall they preach unless they are sent? As it is written: "How beautiful are the feet of those who preach the gospel of peace, Who bring glad tidings of good things!" But they **have not all obeyed the gospel**. For Isaiah says, "Lord, who has believed our report?" So then **faith comes by hearing, and hearing by the word of God**.

But I say, have they not heard? Yes indeed: "Their sound has gone out to all the earth, And their words to the ends of the world." But I say, did Israel not know? First Moses says: "**I will provoke you to jealousy** by those who are not a nation, I will move you to anger by a foolish nation." But Isaiah is very bold and says: "I was found by those who did not seek Me; I was made manifest to those who did not ask for Me." But to Israel he says: "All day long I have stretched out My hands to a **disobedient and contrary people**." **Rom. 10:1-21**

YOUR PRAYER FOR SALVATION AND DELIVERANCE:

"Father, I thank You for Your word of truth regarding rebellion and disobedience. The truth of Your word has opened my eyes to see how these sins have grieved Your heart. Lord, with all my heart I am sorry for the sin of rebellion and disobedience. I repent for every sin in my life and I ask for Your forgiveness today. I renounce every idol that I ever served and I grant that place to You only as Lord of my heart. I ask that You would please purge every dead work through Your Holy Spirit, who is Your promise You sent to me, so I can live a godly and holy life before You. I cannot do this on my own, I need You so desperately. Please wash me with Your precious holy blood from every sin and cleanse me from all unrighteousness as I call upon Jesus now.

Lord Jesus, please come into my heart and be the Lord of my life. I declare You as my Lord and Savior today. I ask forgiveness for my sins as I forgive and release every person who has ever offended me. Forgive me Lord for holding unforgiveness and save my soul, I pray. Please fill me with the person of the Holy Spirit, who You promised to me, to help me live my life in a way that pleases You. Thank you Jesus for coming in and I declare that I will live for You and serve You all the days of my life.

Thank You Jesus for coming in, thank You for sending Your Holy Spirit to live in me and thank You for saving my soul granting me eternal life with You, amen."

My prayer for you: Father, thank You for my new brother/sister in Christ. Fill them up to overflowing with Your presence and peace I pray and manifest Yourself to them daily as they surrendered and dedicated their life to You. I pray abundance in every area of their life in Jesus' Name, and thank You for cleansing them spirit soul and body, in Jesus' name, amen.

THE FATHER'S PROMISE TO YOU, THE HOLY SPIRIT

"Behold, I send the Promise of My Father upon you; but tarry in the city of Jerusalem until you are endued with power from on high." Lk. 24:49

"And being assembled together with them, He commanded them not to depart from Jerusalem, but to wait for the Promise of the Father, "which, He said, "you have heard from Me; for John truly baptized with water, **but** you shall be baptized with the Holy Spirit not many days from now." Therefore, when they had come together, they asked Him, saying, "Lord, will You at this time restore the kingdom to Israel?" And He said to them, "It is not for you to know times or seasons which the Father has put in His own authority. But **you shall receive power when the Holy Spirit has come upon you; and you shall be witnesses to Me in Jerusalem, and in all Judea and Samaria, and to the end of the earth**." **Acts 1:4-8**

Jesus said, "But when the Helper comes, whom I shall send to you from the Father, the Spirit of truth who proceeds from the Father, **He will testify of Me**. And you also will bear witness, because you have been with Me from the beginning." **Jn. 15:26-27**

"But now I go away to Him who sent Me, and none of you asks Me, 'Where are You going?' But because I have said these things to you, sorrow has filled your heart. Nevertheless I tell you the truth. **It is to your advantage that I go away; for if I do not go away, the Helper will not come to you; but if I depart, I will send Him to you**. And when He has come, He will **convict the world of sin, and of righteousness, and of judgment**: of sin, **because they do not believe in Me**; of righteousness, **because I go to My Father and you see Me no more**; of judgment, because **the ruler of this world is judged**.

"I still have many things to say to you, but you cannot bear *them* now. However, **when He, the Spirit of truth, has come, He will guide you into all truth; for He will not speak on His own *authority*, but whatever He hears He will speak; and He will tell you things to come. He will glorify Me, for He will take of what is Mine and declare *it* to you.** All things that the Father has are Mine. Therefore I said that **He will take of Mine and declare *it* to you**." **Jn. 16:5-15**

"When the Day of Pentecost had fully come, they were all with one accord in one place. And suddenly there came a sound from heaven, as of a rushing mighty wind, and it filled the whole house where they were sitting. Then there appeared to them divided tongues, as of fire, and *one* sat upon each of them. And they were all filled with the Holy Spirit and began to speak with other tongues, as the Spirit gave them utterance.

And there were dwelling in Jerusalem Jews, devout men, from every nation under heaven. And when this sound occurred, the multitude came together, and were confused, because everyone heard them speak in his own language. Then they were all amazed and marveled, saying to one another, "Look, are not all these who speak Galileans? And how is it that we hear, each in our own language in which we were born? Parthians and Medes and Elamites, those dwelling in Mesopotamia, Judea and Cappadocia, Pontus and Asia, Phrygia and Pamphylia, Egypt and the parts of Libya adjoining Cyrene, visitors from Rome, both Jews and proselytes, Cretans and Arabs—we hear them speaking in our own tongues the wonderful works of God." So they were all amazed and perplexed, saying to one another, "Whatever could this mean?"

Others mocking said, "They are full of new wine." But Peter, standing up with the eleven, raised his voice and said to them, "Men of Judea and all who dwell in Jerusalem, let this be known to you, and heed my words. For these are not drunk, as you suppose, since it is *only* the third hour of the day. But this is what was spoken by the prophet Joel: '<u>And it shall come to pass in the last days, says God, That I will pour out of My Spirit on all flesh; Your</u>

sons and your daughters shall prophesy,
Your young men shall see visions, Your old men shall dream dreams. And **on My menservants and on My maidservants I will pour out My Spirit in those days**; And they shall prophesy.
I will show wonders in heaven above and signs in the earth beneath: Blood and fire and vapor of smoke. The sun shall be turned into darkness, and the moon into blood, Before the coming of the great and awesome day of the Lord.
And it shall come to pass that **whoever** calls on the name of the Lord **shall be saved**.'

"Men of Israel, hear these words: Jesus of Nazareth, a Man attested by God to you by miracles, wonders, and signs which God did through Him in your midst, as you yourselves also know—Him, being delivered by the determined purpose and foreknowledge of God, you have taken by lawless hands, have crucified, and put to death; whom God raised up, having loosed the pains of death, because it was not possible that He should be held by it. For David says concerning Him:

'I foresaw the Lord always before my face, For He is at my right hand, that I may not be shaken.
Therefore my heart rejoiced, and my tongue was glad; Moreover my flesh also will rest in hope. For You will not leave my soul in Hades, Nor will You allow Your Holy One to see corruption.
You have made known to me the ways of life; You will make me **full of joy in Your presence**.'
"Men *and* brethren, let *me* speak freely to you of the patriarch David, that he is both dead and buried, and his tomb is with us to this day. Therefore, being a prophet, and knowing that God had

sworn with an oath to him that of the fruit of his body, according to the flesh, He would raise up the Christ to sit on his throne, he, foreseeing this, spoke concerning the resurrection of the Christ, that His soul was not left in Hades, nor did His flesh see corruption. This Jesus God has raised up, of which we are all witnesses. Therefore being exalted to the right hand of God, and having received **from the Father the promise of the Holy Spirit**, He poured out this which you now see and hear.

"For David did not ascend into the heavens, but he says himself:

'The Lord said to my Lord, "Sit at My right hand, Till I make Your enemies Your footstool." '
"Therefore let all the house of Israel know assuredly that God has made this Jesus, whom you crucified, **both Lord and Christ**."

Now when they heard this, they were **cut to the heart**, and said to Peter and the rest of the apostles, "Men and brethren, what shall we do?"

Then Peter said to them, "Repent, and let every one of you be baptized in the name of Jesus Christ for the remission of sins; and you shall receive the gift of the Holy Spirit. For **the promise** is to you and to your children, and to all who are afar off, as many as the Lord our God will call." **Acts 2:1-38**

WHO IS THE HOLY SPIRIT?

He is mentioned from Genesis to Revelation. He is the Creative Person of the triune Godhead. He physically manifested whatever the Father would speak. He came upon the prophets like Moses, Samuel, Daniel, Elijah, Isaiah and Jeremiah in the Old Testament, speaking to them messages directly from the Father. He dwelt inside Jesus when He was baptized in the River Jordan, John the Baptist, His twelve disciples, Paul and believers everywhere throughout the New Testament. He is called the Paraclete (the one who walks alongside), the Spirit of Truth, the Spirit of Grace, the Comforter and the Intercessor.

HE DWELLS INSIDE US

"But if the Spirit of Him who raised Jesus from the dead dwells in you, He who raised Christ from the dead will also give life to your mortal bodies through His Spirit who dwells in you." **Rom. 8:11**

The Holy Spirit's awesome work begins with His convicting, healing and cleansing power on the inside of our hearts. He will then begin to develop Godly fruit that can be seen in our lives. We only need to give Him the permission to change us. His will reveal the hidden manna in the scriptures to us and bear witness with us that Jesus is alive forevermore!

HE IS THE SPIRIT OF JESUS CHRIST

"For I know that this will turn out for my deliverance through your prayer and the supply of the **Spirit of Jesus Christ,** according to my earnest expectation and hope that in nothing I shall be ashamed, but with all boldness, as always, so now also Christ will be magnified in my body, whether by life or by death." **Phil. 1:19-20**

"By this you know the Spirit of God: Every spirit that confesses that Jesus Christ has come in the flesh is of God, and every spirit that does not confess that Jesus Christ has

come in the flesh is not of God. And this is the <u>*spirit* of the Antichrist</u>, which you have heard was coming, and is now already in the world." 1 Jn. 4:3-4

HE IS THE THIRD PERSON AND FORM OF THE GODHEAD: FATHER, SON AND HOLY SPIRIT and THEY ARE ALL ONE!!!!

"Hear, O Israel: <u>The Lord our God, the Lord *is* one</u>!" Deut. 6:4

<u>CHAPTER 9</u>

<u>IN CONCLUSION</u>

This book contains truth as it all comes from the scriptures. I obeyed the Holy Spirit to release this powerful word of His to you. I pray as you have read it, that the truth contained will not only opened your eyes and heart, but will have such **keeping power through the Holy Spirit** to bring an eternal guidance to your life and walk with Him. It is so very clear to me the difference to our lives through the choice to obey the Lord's word to us. So many people question why so many destructive things take place in their lives. The answer lies between you and God. Seek Him for your answer.

Here is a word He laid on my heart for you: **"And you will seek Me and find Me, when you search for Me with all your heart." Jer. 29:13**

There is an extremely clear <u>spiritual law</u> that is revealed throughout the bible. The law of obedience and the blessing and the law of disobedience and the price tag. I think after you have read all of these verses for yourself, you will

conclude the same.

"We then, as workers together with Him also plead with you not to receive the grace of God in vain. For He says: "In an acceptable time I have heard you, and in the day of salvation I have helped you." Behold, now is the accepted time; behold, now is the day of salvation. We give no offense in anything, that our ministry may not be blamed. But in **all things** we commend ourselves as ministers of God: in much patience, in tribulations, in needs, in distresses, in stripes, in imprisonments, in tumults, in labors, in sleeplessness, in fastings; by purity, by knowledge, by longsuffering, by kindness, by the Holy Spirit, by sincere love, by the word of truth, by the power of God, by the armor of righteousness on the right hand and on the left, by honor and dishonor, by evil report and good report; as deceivers, and yet true; as unknown, and yet well known; as dying, and behold we live; as chastened, and yet not killed; as sorrowful, yet always rejoicing; as poor, yet making many rich; as having nothing, and yet possessing all things." **2 Cor. 6:1-10**

I ask the Lord to bless you and your family with His great wisdom, which will guide your life as you grow in the knowledge of Him and walk daily in His obedience and abundant grace!

"And the Lord spoke to Moses, saying: "Speak to Aaron and his sons, saying, 'This is the way you shall **bless** the children of Israel. Say to them: "The Lord bless you and keep you; The Lord make His face shine upon you, and be gracious to you; the Lord lift up His countenance upon you, and give you peace. So they shall put

My name on the children of Israel, and **<u>I will bless them</u>**."
Num. 6:22-27

There is a short saying that has helped me many times with my <u>life choices</u>:

"GOD'S WAYS, GOD'S RESULTS, EVERY TIME! Please memorize this truth, as it will help guide you in every decision you make.

A Word I hear for you:

"Oh that you would know Me and the power of My might, in the power of My resurrection, in the fullness of My glory and grace. Look to Me, My people. For I am with you wherever you go. My eye is upon you and My heart longs for you to seek after Me and then you <u>will</u> find Me. I will quickly make Myself known to you. I have waited for you and have longed for you to know My heart. I Am the Lord, that is My name, and there is none other besides Me. Come to Me, My beloved child. I love you."

Word of the Lord given to me on 8/27/2018

"That you would know Me and the power of My might, from the governmental head down to the smallest of creation. That you would know the Spirit of Grace and Supplication, the Spirit of Sanctification and Consecration which would begin to manifest the Spirit of Glory in your lives.

Come away and spend quality time with Me. Seek My face, seek to know Me, not just what I can give to you. For I have

riches beyond what you could even imagine. For the true riches of Heaven are found within Me. Riches beyond compare with what you have here. Come away My beloved, Come away!

I will visit America again with great power and great glory. I will show her the power of My might and My heavenly hosts will be dispersed about the land. I will raise up firebrands to declare My word fearlessly in diverse places and I will display My Kingdom and My rulership here in this land. As I had promised many, that will I do.

I will deliver My people who have been under the heavy weight of the oppressor and I will remove their burdens. I will reveal Myself to many and they will know their God and do great exploits. Prepare My people, prepare."

SPEAK THIS DECLARATION TO HIM:

"In You O Lord I put my trust; Let me never be put to shame. Deliver me in Your righteousness and cause me to escape. Incline Your ear to me and save me. Be my strong refuge, to which I may resort continually. You have given the commandment to save me. For You are my rock and my fortress. Deliver me O my God, out of the hand of the wicked; out of the hand of the unrighteous and cruel man. For You are my hope, O Lord God. You are my trust from my youth. By You I have been upheld from birth; You are He who took me out of my mother's womb. My praise shall be continually of You. I have become as a wonder to many. But You are my strong refuge. Let my mouth be filled with Your praise and with Your glory all the day." **Ps. 71:1-8**

“Lord come to me and reveal Yourself to me. I want to know You and walk with You and fulfill Your divine plan for my life every day, Amen.”

ABOUT THE AUTHOR

Diane and her husband Michel are residents of Elberton, Georgia. Diane was born again in 1984 and was a long-term member of The Rock of Sarasota, Florida under the covering of Pastor Richard Brantley for 9 years. She served in the Children's Ministry, Singles Ministry and Set Free Ministries, as well as the Healing Rooms. She also served as Vice President of the Sarasota Chapter of Women's Aglow and currently as a Vice President of Outreach in the Elberton Aglow Community Lighthouse. They currently attend local church at "Celebration Outreach Center" in Elberton, Ga. since 2013, led by Pastor Bill Jones.

Diane is a graduate of Ethnoslink International Ministry Training Center in 2001 and received an Associate's Degree. Michel and Diane lead **CrossSounds Ministries** in Elberton, Ga and are raising up sons and daughters of the kingdom through outreaches with training and equipping, to send the church forth as soul winners, utilizing their ministerial gifts and calling in the Kingdom of God. They also have a gospel tent to reach lost souls. They offer prophetic seminars to assist others to have their own personal encounter with the Lord in a tangible way called "The Beauty of the King." Lives have been dramatically changed because of these 2-day seminars. She has authored 3 other books: "Jesus Breaks the Chain of Offense", "The Beauty of the King" and "Breaking the Chains of Addiction". All of the books contain personal testimonies and are loaded with the word of God that brings deliverance and healing.

We have one goal in mind and that is to simply obey our King, whatever He says and whatever He desires to do in and through us. If you would like to schedule a "Beauty of the King" Prophetic Seminar or need to contact us: **Dianeb22000@gmail.com**

CrossSounds Website:

www.CrossSounds.org

CrossSounds Ministries Gospel Tent